IN THE KNOW IN THE

U.S.A.

LIVING LANGUAGE®

TERRA COGNITA™

Also available from

LIVING LANGUAGE®
A Random House Company

American English Pronunciation Program

Better pronunciation means better communication. Improve your foreign or regional accent with this easy, prac~~
pronunci~~
out all the
cassettes
0-609-6041

The Pri

amed
grams
Eng-
work,
grams
es to

Grammar
sounding
0-609-8111

scary-

Word Sn
misused
0-609-811

ently

Word S
to do we
0-609-811

know

Word S
and cha
0-609-811

esting

The *Wo*
vocabul
instruct
0-609-811

urs of
mmar

Available at bookstores everywhere.
www.livinglanguage.com

300 West 49th Street Suite 314 New York, New York 10019 USA
Phone: 212.663.9890 Fax: 212.663.2404
E-mail: info@terracognita.com
www.terracognita.com

Know Your World

Terra Cognita provides top quality cross-cultural training service and resources. The goal of our cross-cultural learning material is to help you build the awareness and skills to recognize and respect cultural differences you will encounter. Terra Cognita programs thereby ensure a sucessful adjustment to life in a new culture for expatriates and the skills necessary to succeed in international business.

Terra Cognita delivers cross-cultural learning with private seminars and workshops, with online learning modules, and with a variety of video, audio and printed material. Currently Terra Cognita programs meet the needs of expatriates and international business colleagues at various multinational companies, government agencies and educational institutions worldwide.

 LIVE ABROAD! is an innovative video-based expatriate preparation program that covers the entire expatriate experience from preparing to go through the cultural adjustment process to the final return home.

 WORK ABROAD! is a video-based program that explains and vividly recreates the cross-cultural dynamics of the international business environment.

For more information on Terra Cognita
and a wealth of articles and resources for cross-cultural learning,
visit our Web site at WWW.TERRACOGNITA.COM

V I D E O S   S E M I N A R S   O N L I N E

LIVING LANGUAGE®
A Random House Company

IN THE KNOW IN THE

U.S.A.

THE INDISPENSABLE GUIDE TO WORKING AND LIVING IN THE UNITED STATES

WRITTEN BY

Jennifer Phillips

EDITED BY

Suzanne McQuade

Terra Cognita

Copyright © 2003 by Living Language, A Random House Company

Living Language is a member of the Random House Information Group.

Living Language and colophon are registered trademarks of Random House, Inc.

Maps © Fodors LLC

Fodor's is a registered trademark of Random House, Inc.

Published in the United States by Living Language, A Random House Company

www.livinglanguage.com

Editor: Suzanne McQuade
Production Editor: Marina Padakis
Production Manager: Pat Ehresmann
Interior Design: Barbara Bachman
Illustrations: Adrian Hashimi

First Edition

ISBN 0-609-61113-5

Library of Congress Cataloging-in-Publication Data available upon request.

PRINTED IN THE UNITED STATES OF AMERICA

10 9 8 7 6 5 4 3 2 1

ACKNOWLEDGMENTS

Thanks to the many people who generously shared their experiences and ideas to make this book come together. A special thanks to my editor, Suzanne McQuade, for her expert guidance and patience.

And thanks to the rest of the Living Language team: Lisa Alpert, Elizabeth Bennett, Chris Warnasch, Zviezdana Verzich, Helen Tang, Pat Ehresmann, Denise De Gennaro, Linda Schmidt, Marina Padakis, Sophie Chin, Barbara Bachman, and Rita Wuebbeler.

CONTENTS

W hether you're moving to the United States or traveling there for business, it's essential that you know what to expect and what will be expected of you. Cross-cultural awareness provides you with just that knowledge. *In the Know in the USA* is designed to help business people and their families navigate the often complex waters of life in another culture. By culture we don't mean a Broadway play or a look into the American jazz scene. Culture is the backdrop of every activity you engage in and every word you exchange. In the United States, you'll be dealing with a foreign culture every time you shake a colleague's hand, sit down to write an e-mail, get on a train, or even buy a loaf of bread. A list of "dos & don'ts" provides only part of the picture. A more thorough understanding of culture—what really motivates people's behaviors, attitudes, beliefs, and habits—will allow you, and any family members with you, to adapt with ease to both the social and business environments of the United States.

This book was developed to be easy, practical, and comprehensive. First, you'll get an overview of some general background information about the United States, such as its history, geography, political system, and social structure. This is no history text, though. The "Background" chapter is meant to be a brief survey that will familiarize you with some important landmarks you'll no doubt hear about or see. If something strikes you as interesting, the "Background" section will also serve you well as a way to get started in a particular area; we leave any further exploration of American history to you.

Next, you'll read an overview of American culture. For our purposes here, we've broken culture down into the following six categories: time, communication, group dynamics, status & hierarchy, relationships, and reasoning. Naturally, this provides only a general picture of the components of American culture, but a very practical picture, too. And even while using these generalizations, we can never forget that any culture is made up of individuals, and individuals vary. Learning about these important general concepts, where differences and pitfalls abound, will better prepare you and your family for a more successful experience in the United States.

The next section, "Living Abroad: Thoughts Before You Go," is meant to give you some insight about the issues that people face when they are immersed in another culture. Here you'll learn what to expect as a businessperson, a family member, a parent, a child, an individual, or a teenager. This section applies to life in any other culture, and you'll find the insight invaluable. It will raise the kind of important questions you'll want to consider when preparing to make an adjustment to life in the United States. Most importantly, it will prepare you to face some tough challenges and then to reap some wonderful benefits.

The next two sections of the book, "Getting Around" and "Living and Staying in the United States," are comprehensive, step-by-step guides to everyday life in the United States. These are the issues that everyone must deal with, from driving and taking buses to shopping to social etiquette. These sections are full of easily organized information, practical lists, and essential tips. Everyone—single traveler, parent, or child—will benefit.

Next are two sections designed specifically for the businessperson. In "Business Environment," you'll get an idea of the general principles that govern working in the United States, from company values and structure to chain of command, unions, workspace, and women in business. In the next chapter, "Business Step-by-Step," you'll learn about the real essentials of doing business in the United States, ranging from such important issues as speeches and presentations, negotiations, and dress to such often overlooked but crucial details as business card etiquette and making appointments.

Finally, we leave you with an introduction to the business essentials of the English language. This is no full-service language course;

you won't be memorizing any irregular verbs or grammar rules. But you'll find that the minimal amount of time it takes to learn some basic business expressions and vocabulary will be recouped a hundred times over. Your American colleagues and friends will be very appreciative that you've made an effort to learn just a little of their language.

Good luck, and enjoy! We hope you find this coverage informative, practical, and enriching.

BACKGROUND

The United States is considered a world leader whose policies and actions are felt not only at home but abroad as well.

The "culture" of America has seeped well beyond its own borders as American products, music, fashions, and even fast food have appeared in the most unlikely of places. Many newcomers to the United States feel that they already know about America and Americans because they have read so much about it in their newspapers, seen it in movies, heard it from the latest international pop diva—and, of course, seen or even met American tourists! These represent only bits and pieces of America, and many people are astonished at the complexity of the American culture when they arrive to live and work there.

One of the issues that Americans deal with when they are working with the international community is what to call themselves. At various times critics have pointed out that all citizens of both North and South America have the right to call themselves "Americans," and that it is typical of the arrogance of the United States to usurp this term. Even more extreme are those who argue that even the use of "United States" is somewhat presumptive in light of the fact that one of the United States's closest neighbors, Mexico, includes those same words in its official name, Estados Unidos Mexicanos (United Mexican States). Taken together, those two arguments leave the people of the United States with no practical names that are guaranteed not to offend someone. The only reasonable solution seems to be the original one: With all respect to the cohabitants of all countries in North and South America, this book uses "United States" and "America" to refer to the country and "Americans" to refer to its people.

By the time you finish this book, you will have learned much about Americans and, hopefully, even about yourself. But for now, let's start with the basics.

VITAL STATISTICS

Official Name	**United States of America**
Capital	**Washington, D.C. (District of Columbia)**
Federal Flag	**13 alternating red and white stripes (representing the 13 original colonies) with a blue square in the upper left corner with 50 white stars (representing the 50 states)**
National Anthem	**"Star-Spangled Banner"**
Area	**9,629,091 sq km/3,618,000 sq mi**
Land Distribution	**arable land: 19%; permanent crops: 0%; permanent pastures: 25%; forests and woodland: 30%; other: 26%**

Highest Point	Mount McKinley, Alaska (6,194 m/20,320 ft)
Lowest Point	Death Valley, California (-86 m/-282 ft)
Natural Resources	coal, copper, lead, molybdenum, phosphates, uranium, bauxite, gold, iron, mercury, nickel, potash, silver, tungsten, zinc, petroleum, natural gas, timber
Population (2000)	281,421,906
Population Growth (2000 est.)	0.91%
Ethnicity (based on 2000 census)	white 75.1%, black 12.3%, Asian 3.6%, American Indian or Alaskan Native 0.9%, other 5.6% , bi- or multiracial 2.4%1
Language	English2
Literacy	97%
Religions	Protestant 55%, Roman Catholic 28%, Jewish 2%, other 7%, none 8%
Currency	U.S. Dollar (1 dollar = 100 cents)
GDP (2000)	$9.963 trillion
Major Trading Partners	Canada, Mexico, Japan
Inflation (2000)	3.4%
Employment by Industry	services 80%; industry 18%; agriculture 2%
Unemployment (2000)	4.0%

[1] The United States Census Bureau considers Latinos and Hispanics to be people of Latin American descent who are of any ethnic background (white, black, or Asian). People of Latin American descent are not categorized separately. A supplementary question in the 2000 census revealed that 12.5% of the population is Hispanic or Latino.

[2] Spanish is an important secondary language, spoken at home by about 7% of the population.

GEOGRAPHY AND CLIMATE

The United States is a vast and geographically varied country. The continental United States (excluding Alaska and Hawaii) stretches across 2,800 miles (4,500 kilometers) and four time zones; there are six hours separating the east coast and Hawaii. Driving from coast to coast would take you about five days by car—more if you stop to see any of the sights. Along the way, you would pass through one-stop-light towns and sprawling metropolises; and over rolling green hills and barren, rocky mountains; and through fertile farmland and arid deserts. The climates in the United States vary greatly, from tropical Hawaii to frozen Alaska, from the western deserts to the rainy northwest. Indeed, it's not uncommon to see up to a 70-degree (Fahrenheit) difference between the coldest and warmest temperatures measured in the United States.

Although it is difficult to describe the geography and climate of the United States in a few simple words, the continental states can generally be divided into seven regions: the Atlantic/Gulf Coastal Plains, the Appalachian Highlands, the Interior Plains, the Interior Highlands, the Rocky Mountains, the Intermontane Region, and the Pacific Mountains. Alaska and Hawaii, because of their distance from the rest of the states, have unique geographies and climates.

Extending along the eastern and southeastern coasts, the Atlantic and Gulf Coastal Plains merge in Florida. This area is marked with many rivers, harbors, islands, and beaches. Rising from the coastal plains are the Appalachian Mountains, an ancient mountain range worn by eons of erosion, which demarcate the Appalachian Highland region. The Appalachians stretch from southeastern Canada down to Alabama.

Moving west brings one to the Interior Plains and Interior Highlands. The highlands begin just west of the Mississippi River, forming the Ozark and Ouachita mountain ranges. The plains contain the fertile central lowlands, which are the nation's heart of agriculture, and the Great Plains, a plateau that rises to the foothills of the Rocky Mountains.

The country's youngest mountain system is the Rocky Mountains, which extend from Canada to New Mexico. Running along the crest of the Rockies is the Continental Divide, a geographical feature separating the country into two parts: areas east of the Continental Divide drain into the Atlantic Ocean, areas west drain into the Pacific Ocean.

Between the Rocky Mountains and the Pacific Mountains to the west lies the Intermontane Region, an arid stretch of plateaus and basins. This area contains the Grand Canyon, one of the seven natural wonders of the world, and Death Valley, the country's lowest point. Before the land meets the Pacific Ocean, it rises again into mountains. The Pacific Mountains are a series of ranges paralleling the coast, including the Cascade Mountains and the Sierra Nevada range, which contains Mt. Whitney, the continental United States's highest point.

Finally, the land reaches the ocean in the Pacific coastal area, another series of mountain ranges. The San Andreas Fault runs parallel to these ranges from San Francisco to Mexico, making earthquakes a common occurrence. The coastal plain on the western coast is narrow; in fact, in many areas the mountains meet the sea face-to-face.

Alaska's geography is almost as diverse as that of the continental states. Alaska itself can be divided into four regions: the Artic Lowlands, the Rocky Mountains, the Central Basin and Highlands, and the Pacific Mountains. Mt. McKinley, the highest point in the United States, is located in the Rocky Mountains in Alaska. The islands that are found to the southeast of Alaska are part of the Aleutian Island chain and were originally part of the Pacific Mountain system. There is volcanic activity and earthquakes throughout these islands.

Hawaii lies on the tops of volcanoes that rise from the Pacific Ocean. Hawaii has two active volcanoes, Mauna Kea and Mauna Loa; the rest are inactive.

PEOPLE AND LIFE

The United States is a place with as much diversity in its people as in its geography. Like the geographical divisions, the cultural differences can be divided into general regions. However, before moving on to regional differences, it is worth reviewing the history of the people of the United States.

Native Americans

The original inhabitants of the North American continent are thought to be hunters who arrived from Asia by way of a land bridge across the Bering Strait, a migration that began some 20,000 years ago. When Christopher Columbus arrived in the "New World" in 1492, he mistakenly believed himself to be in the Indies (the medieval name for Asia), and called the people he found living in this new land "Indians."

After twenty centuries of living in North America, the Native American population was decimated in a matter of only 200 years as Europeans began immigrating to the "New World." Along with their hopes and dreams, these Europeans brought with them territorial wars, and diseases against which the Native Americans had no immunity. In this short period of time, the European immigrants forced the native people into smaller and smaller corners as they pushed west. In the 19th century, the U.S. government sought to control the "Indian problem" by forcing tribes onto reservations, specific plots of land set aside for them. However, this land was generally in places that were virtually unusable for crops, and Native Americans were unable to sustain their populations. This meant that the Native Americans became dependent on government assistance, and today, many of those who live on reservations live in poverty. As a result of the encroachment of the newcomers, some tribes disappeared altogether; others lost their languages and much of their cultures. Today there are around 2 million Native Americans, only 0.9% of the country's population; about one third of Native Americans live on reservations.

Immigrants

With the exception of Native Americans, most Americans are newcomers to the country, especially when compared to the centuries-old cultures of the rest of the world. People came to the United States in search of freedom, opportunity, and even adventure. English prevailed as the language of the new world because the English were the dominant ethnic group among the early settlers. However, the mid-1800s saw wave after wave of immigration from Europe because of poor harvest and famine, political unrest, and war. Notable trends in immigration included the surge of Irish immigrants in the late 1840s as a direct result of a blight on the potato crops in Ireland that left many starving. The latter years of the decade also saw a wave of German immigrants following an internal war in Germany. In fact, many immigrants fought in the American Civil War in the 1860s, responding to the federal government's offer of land grants in return for service in the Union army. Today 14% of the population has Irish ancestry and 22% descend from German immigrants.

The late 1880s brought large numbers of Jews to the United States as they fled persecution in eastern Europe. The American Jewish population currently numbers more than 5 million.

If you had immigrated to the United States between 1892 and 1954, you would most likely have arrived at Ellis Island, a special entry port opened by the government to handle the overwhelming number of immigrants. During its 62 years of service, Ellis Island, under the Statue of Liberty's watchful gaze, was the doorway to America for some 12 million immigrants. Situated just beside Ellis Island, the Statue of Liberty, a gift given to the American people by France in 1886, welcomed immigrants to their new homeland, lighting the way with her glowing torch. The base of the Statue of Liberty bears the words of poet Emma Lazarus:

> *Give me your tired, your poor,*
> *Your huddled masses yearning to breathe free,*
> *The wretched refuse of your teeming shore.*
> *Send these, the homeless, tempest-tossed to me,*
> *I lift my lamp beside the golden door!*

The United States has long been called a melting pot, and indeed for decades, most immigrants adapted by giving up some of their own cultural customs and their languages. For example, children born to immigrants were usually encouraged to use English only; each generation became further removed from their forefathers' languages. However, in recent years, the melting pot has become a salad bowl, where rather than shed their own cultures, people embrace American culture while retaining much of their own language and customs.

Slaves

In stark contrast to the immigrants who came willingly are the hundreds of thousands of Africans who were brought to America as slaves. The practice of slavery began early in America's history, in the 1600s, and did not end until 1808, when slave trade became illegal. It is important to note, however, that although it was no longer legal to import slaves, slave ownership continued for almost six decades, especially in southern states, which depended on slave labor to work the fields.

Even after slavery was abolished, slaves faced segregation and racism, and were considered by many people to be inferior. They did not immediately gain the rights that white Americans had, such as the right to vote, and they were further limited by poor education. Indeed, segregation remained legal until the 1950s; unfortunately, we have yet to eradicate other forms of discrimination and racism. Some 12.3% of the American population today is African American.

Regional Differences

Any attempt to characterize the people of a country or region runs the risk of stereotyping. However, Americans themselves assign various characteristics to people from other parts of the country. Regional differences show up in accents and language patterns, in the food that appears on breakfast and dinner tables, and in more intangible things such as the pace of life. These differences result from many things, including immigration patterns, economic factors, regional histories, and, some would say, even the climate!

The lines of regional differences are generally drawn along state lines. There are seven recognizable regions, although there is nothing official about them and there is some room for discussion on which states are part of which regions. Of course, the following characterizations do not apply to everyone; you will find a diverse range of people wherever you go.

New England

New England is the designation for the northeastern most states and includes Maine, New Hampshire, Vermont, Massachusetts, Connecticut, and Rhode Island. New Englanders have a reputation for being hardworking but taciturn. New England is where many wealthy families live or have second homes; a visitor to Newport, Rhode Island, can see, and even tour, the "summer cottages" of the Astors, Vanderbilts, and other well-to-do families. It is also home to some of America's "royalty," such as the Kennedys. New England is famous for its seafood and chowders. There are various accents in the region, but Boston in particular is renowned for its unique pronunciations. For example, "park" becomes "pahk" and "car" becomes "cah," while "idea" become "idear" and "pizza" becomes "pizzer."

Mid-Atlantic

Adjoining the New England states on the south are the Mid-Atlantic states of New York, New Jersey, Pennsylvania, Delaware, and Maryland. New York City and its characteristics tend to overshadow the Mid-Atlantic states. In this booming metropolis, the pace of life is frantic, and everything revolves around business. Other cities and towns are not as hectic. Pennsylvania, for example, is home to the oldest Amish settlement in North America. The Amish are a religious group who remain separated from the modern world, eschewing modern inventions such as automobiles.

South

The Southern states extend from Virginia to Florida and west to Texas and Oklahoma. Other states in this region are West Virginia, Kentucky, Tennessee, North Carolina, South Carolina, Georgia, Alabama, Mississippi, Arkansas, and Louisiana. Caricatures of Southerners are painted with two brushes: that of the Southern belle or gentleman, oozing politeness, hospitality, and southern charm, and that of the Southern "redneck," a hard-drinking, rather crude "good ol' boy" (the name "redneck" comes from the sunburn one gets on one's neck from working in the hot sun; the term is often used derogatorily). The former represents the upper echelons of the social classes, the latter represents the lower or working classes. The Southern drawl is very distinctive, but can be difficult to understand. Speech patterns are slower, words are more drawn out, many consonants are softened, and final consonants are often dropped. For example, "where" is more like "whe-uh" and "going" becomes "goin'."

Midwest

Lying in the middle of the country are the Midwestern states of Ohio, Michigan, Indiana, Wisconsin, Illinois, Minnesota, Iowa, Missouri, North Dakota, South Dakota, Nebraska, and Kansas. The Midwest is known as America's heartland. Here you will find fields of corn and wheat as far as the eye can see. Consequently, the stereotype of the Midwesterner is that of the farmer: honest and hardworking with a more simple life. The English spoken in the Midwest is considered "standard" for the United States. With the notable exception of the Scandinavian-influenced Michigan, Minnesota, and Wisconsin accents, it is flatter and without the accents found elsewhere. This is the English that you will hear on the nightly news; most broadcasters are trained to emulate the Midwestern accent—or lack of an accent.

New Mexico, Arizona, and parts of Utah, Nevada, and California make up the American Southwest. Much of the Southwest is desert dotted with green oases. It is home to some of America's most spectacular natural wonders, such as the Grand Canyon and the Painted Desert. There is a strong Native American influence as well as the flavor of Mexico in some areas, reflected in the architecture, in the food, and elsewhere. People in the Southwest are viewed as more relaxed and easygoing than their frantic East Coast counterparts, largely due to the influence of Mexican and Native American cultures in that area as well as extremely hot temperatures, which encourage a slower pace.

W e s t

The Western states are Colorado, Wyoming, Montana, Utah, California, Nevada, Idaho, Oregon, and Washington. The American West calls to mind the frontier spirit and conjures up the ghosts of settlers pushing west in search of land, gold, and opportunity, and of cowboys riding the ranges. There is a diverse mosaic of people in this area, from the calloused rancher to the glamorous Hollywood star. Like Southwesterners, folks in the West have a reputation for being more laid-back than their East Coast fellows, while Californians are also thought to lead more outlandish lifestyles.

A l a s k a / H a w a i i

Although Alaska and Hawaii are as different as their climates, they are often grouped together as the only two states that are not part of the continental United States. Both, however, have retained strong influences from their native peoples.

Alaska is America's largest state but its least populated. About

15% of the people living in Alaska are Native Americans, mostly Eskimo (also called Inuit; this term includes a number of smaller distinct groups with similar languages and customs) and Aleut. Eskimos and Aleuts are racially similar to native Siberians, and their languages are branches of the Eskimo-Aleut language family. The traditional picture of Eskimos wandering in nomad-like fashion, using harpoons to fish is largely a thing of the past. Today most Eskimos live in settled communities and work for wages; guns have replaced more traditional hunting tools. Aleuts, however, continue to live in relative isolation.

Hawaii includes perhaps more ethnic groups than any other state. The first settlers of the Hawaiian islands were Polynesian travelers. However, starting in the mid-19th century, Chinese, Filipino, Korean, Portuguese, German, Japanese, and Puerto Rican immigrants became part of the Hawaiian landscape. Hawaii's climate and the beauty of its islands, from fierce volcanoes to majestic waves, have made it a vacation paradise. Hawaiians are generally regarded as warm and friendly, taking life at a slower pace than their mainland countrymen.

AMERICAN HISTORY IN BRIEF

The United States has quite a lot of history packed into five centuries, from the arrival of European explorers to independence to assuming a global leadership role. The following outline is an overview of the highlights in American history. History buffs can find shelves of books on the history of the United States in libraries and bookstores, and there are many Internet sites devoted to the topic.

| 1492 | **Christopher Columbus, sailing under the Spanish flag, discovers the Americas for Europe. Contrary to popular myth, Columbus never landed in the current-day United States.** |

1499	Amerigo Vespucci (who lent his name to the Americas) arrives in the New World and explores much of the Northern shores of South America and the islands.
1513	Ponce de León of Spain lands in America, naming the region Florida.
1541	Hernando de Soto of Spain discovers the Mississippi River.
1565	St. Augustine, the oldest permanent settlement in the United States, is founded by Spaniards.
1607	The first permanent settlement by the English in the New World is made at Jamestown, Virginia; Virginia becomes the first of 13 English colonies.
1619	The first representative assembly in America, the House of Burgesses, meets in Virginia.
1620	The Pilgrims on the ship *Mayflower* found a settlement at Plymouth, Massachusetts.
1682	Robert La Salle explores the lower Mississippi Valley and claims the region for France.
1733	Georgia, the 13th English colony, is founded.
1754–63	French and Indian War between France and England in America; Treaty of Paris ends the war and England becomes supreme power in North America; Louisiana ceded to Spain; Florida ceded to Britain.
1773	The Boston Tea Party is the first act of rebellion against Britain following the passing of a new act by the British Parliament taxing tea. Boston patriots, dressed as Indians, board British ships in Boston harbor and dump 342 chests of tea into the water.
1775	The American Revolution begins as the first shots are fired between American colonists and British soldiers on April 19; on June 15, George Washington is chosen as Commander-in-Chief of the Continental Army.

1776	The Declaration of Independence is adopted. General George Washington crosses the Delaware River to fight at Trenton, New Jersey.
1781	Washington accepts the surrender of the British general Cornwallis at Yorktown, Virginia. The Articles of Confederation form the first independent government of the United States of America.
1783	Peace treaty with Britain formally ends the Revolutionary War.
1788	The United States Constitution is ratified by 9 out of 13 states.
1789	The new United States government goes into effect. George Washington is inaugurated as the president; Congress meets in New York City for the first time.
1791	The Bill of Rights (the first 10 amendments) are added to the Constitution.

1800	The national capital is moved from Philadelphia, Pennsylvania, to Washington, D.C.
1803	The Louisiana Purchase (from France) increases the boundaries of the United States.
1812–14	War of 1812 between the United States and Britain; United States maintains its independence.
1836	Texas wins its independence from Mexico.
1846–48	Mexican War; United States gains possession of California and New Mexico.
1860	Abraham Lincoln is elected president; South Carolina secedes from the Union.
1861	Confederate States of America formed by 11 Southern states; Civil War begins.
1863	Union (Northern) forces win decisive battles at Gettysburg, Vicksburg, and Chattanooga. The Emancipation Proclamation takes effect, freeing all slaves in territories at war with the Union.
1864	General William Sherman of the Union forces captures Atlanta and marches across Georgia, while General Ulysses S. Grant closes in on Richmond, Virginia.
1865	Confederate general Robert E. Lee surrenders to Grant at Appomattox Court House, Virginia, ending the Civil War. Lincoln is assassinated as he watches a play in Ford's Theater.
1867	Reconstruction Acts impose military rule on the South following its defeat in the Civil War. Alaska is purchased from Russia.
1868	President Andrew Johnson becomes the first president to be impeached, for violating the Tenure of Office Act. By the virtue of one vote, he retains the presidency.
1876	The telephone is invented by Alexander Graham Bell. Centennial Exposition in Philadelphia celebrates the 100th birthday of the United States.

1877	The withdrawal of last Union troops from the South ends Reconstruction period.
1879	The first practical electric light is invented by Thomas A. Edison.
1884–85	The first skyscraper, the Home Insurance Building, is erected in Chicago, Illinois.
1896	Henry Ford's first car is driven on the streets of Detroit, Michigan.
1898	United States wins the Spanish–American War and takes possession of the Spanish territories of the Philippines (which later gained its independence in 1946), Puerto Rico, and Guam.
1903	Orville and Wilbur Wright succeed in the first air flight in Kitty Hawk, North Carolina.
1914	World War I breaks out in Europe. President Wilson appeals for neutrality in the United States.
1917	Germany begins open submarine warfare; the U.S. declares war against Germany.
1918–19	Armistice ends war; President Wilson attends Paris Peace Conference of victorious nations.
1920	19th Amendment to the Constitution gives women the right to vote.
1929	The stock market reaches new highs, then crashes, precipitating the Great Depression.
1932	Franklin D. Roosevelt elected president and launches the New Deal, a plan for economic reform.
1939	Germany invades Poland, starting World War II. United States declares neutrality.
1941	Japan attacks American forces in Pearl Harbor, bringing the United States into World War II.
1945	Germany surrenders May 8; Japan surrenders September 2. The Cold War begins between the United States and the Soviet Union.

1950	United States joins other United Nations (UN) members in sending military forces to the aid of the Republic of Korea as the Korean War develops.
1952	Republican Dwight D. Eisenhower elected as president, ending 20 years of Democratic governance.
1953	Korean War ends.
1954	Racial segregation of public schools is declared illegal by Supreme Court.
1959	Alaska and Hawaii join the Union as the 49th and 50th states, respectively.
1961	The Central Intelligence Agency (CIA) is involved in unsuccessful invasion of Cuba at Bay of Pigs. First American makes space flight.
1962	Cuban Missile Crisis erupts; Americans prepare for nuclear war before Soviets remove missiles from Cuba.
1963	March on Washington takes place to promote racial equality. President John F. Kennedy is assassinated in Dallas, Texas.
1965	United States sends combat forces to Vietnam.
1968	Assassinations of Martin Luther King Jr., and Senator Robert F. Kennedy provoke race riots around the country.
1969	United States astronauts become the first men to walk on the moon.
1970	Four students at Kent State University in Ohio are killed by the National Guard during anti-Vietnam War protest.
1973	United States withdraws troops from Vietnam.
1974	Watergate scandal and threat of impeachment force President Richard Nixon to resign.
1985	Summit conference between President Ronald Reagan and Soviet leader Mikhail Gorbachev in Geneva, Switzerland, signals the gradual ending of the Cold War.

1990–91	Troops sent to Saudi Arabia in response to Iraq's invasion of Kuwait.
1999	President William Jefferson Clinton becomes the second president in American history to be impeached. The Senate acquits the president on charges of perjury and obstruction of justice.
2001	President George W. Bush inaugurated. Terrorist attacks on the World Trade Center in New York City and the Pentagon in Washington, D.C., lead to military strikes against the Taliban regime and al Qaeda forces in Afghanistan.

NOTED AMERICANS

There are so many people who are important to the history of the United States that it is virtually impossible to separate out only a few. This is not meant to be a conclusive list of important American figures; it merely spotlights some of the people throughout America's history who are especially noteworthy. If you want to learn more about the people who have made their marks on America's past and present, you can find a variety of history books and biographies at a local library or bookstore or on the Internet.

Politics

GEORGE WASHINGTON (1732–1799)

Born in Virginia in 1732, George Washington is called one of the Founding Fathers of the United States of America and was the country's first president. Prior to the American Revolution, Washington was instrumental in western expansion as a surveyor. As a lieutenant colonel in the militia, Washington also fought in the French and Indian War. When the United States began its bid for independence from England, Washington was elected commander in chief of the newly formed but ill-trained army. Washington led U.S. troops through may hard-fought battles in the six-year campaign against the British army. The American Revolution ended in 1781 when British general Cornwallis surrendered to Washington at Yorktown, Virginia. Following the war, Washington helped shape a Constitution for the newly independent country, and in 1787, he was unanimously elected as president.

ABRAHAM LINCOLN (1809–1865)

Abraham Lincoln in many ways embodies the spirit of America. He was born in 1809 in Kentucky into an undistinguished family; it was his ambition, not his family's influence or money, that brought him to the presidency and earned him a place in American history. Lincoln spent many years as a farmhand, a storekeeper, and an army captain before becoming a lawyer and, eventually, a politician. He spent eight years in the Illinois legislature before being elected as the country's 16th president.

In 1860, immediately after Lincoln was elected president, South Carolina seceded from the Union. The next year saw the beginning of the American Civil War. In 1863, Lincoln issued the Emancipation Proclamation, the first step toward freeing all slaves, including those in Confederate states, although the war continued until 1865. Just five days after the Confederate (Southern) army surrendered to the Union (Northern) army, Abraham Lincoln was assassinated at Ford's Theater in Washington, D.C., by John Wilkes Booth.

FRANKLIN DELANO ROOSEVELT (1882–1945)

Born into a wealthy, well-established family, Franklin Delano Roosevelt studied at two of America's most prestigious universities, Harvard and Columbia, before beginning a career as a lawyer. He was elected to the New York State Senate in 1910 and served as Secretary of the Navy from 1913 to 1920. In 1921, Roosevelt was stricken with poliomyelitis while on a summer vacation; he was paralyzed from the waist down. Despite this disability, he returned to politics with renewed vigor, winning the governorship of New York in 1928.

In 1932, Franklin Roosevelt became the country's 32nd president in a landslide victory and eventually served an unprecedented four terms. He entered the White House at the height of crisis, faced with an economy that was in danger of collapse as a result of the Great Depression. In his inaugural address, his now-famous quote, " . . . the only thing we have to fear is fear itself," reverberated throughout the land, bringing hope to a country devastated by poverty and unemployment. Roosevelt acted immediately to enact measures (collectively called the New Deal) to bolster the failing economy, pulling America from the depths of economic recession.

Roosevelt's third term in office saw the beginning of World War II. In 1945, as the war drew to a close, Roosevelt died from a cerebral hemorrhage.

JOHN F. KENNEDY (1917–1963)

The 35th American president, John F. Kennedy was the youngest man—and the first Catholic—elected president. He was also the youngest to die in office. Born in Massachusetts in 1917, Kennedy graduated from Harvard University and entered the navy, where he served during World War II. Following the war, Kennedy was elected to Congress, then to the Senate. In 1960, Kennedy narrowly won the presidency in a race against Richard Nixon. His inaugural address included the memorable phrase, "Ask not what your country can do for you—ask what you can do for your country." During his presidency, Kennedy put into motion programs that led to great economic growth and increased civil rights; his reforms accelerated the space program, brought federal aid to education, and improved Social Security benefits. Kennedy's administration brought a new idealism to the country, but it ended prematurely. In 1963, as he rode in a motorcade through Dallas, Texas, Kennedy was shot and killed by Lee Harvey Oswald.

MARTIN LUTHER KING JR. (1929–1968)

No one has had more impact on America's collective consciousness than Martin Luther King Jr. The son of a Baptist pastor in Atlanta,

Georgia, King was himself a minister and a firm believer in non-violent resistance. He soon became a prominent leader in the Civil Rights movement, leading the 1955–1956 boycott of segregated city bus lines in Montgomery, Alabama, which in turn led to desegregation of buses. He led protests throughout the South and spearheaded the 1963 March on Washington, bringing more than 200,000 people together in support of civil rights. King was awarded the Nobel Peace Prize for his work in 1964. Tragically in 1968, as he stood on the balcony of the Lorraine Motel in Memphis, Tennessee, King was shot and killed by James Earl Ray.

Other important names: Susan B. Anthony (suffragette), Thomas Jefferson (former president), Rosa Parks (civil rights activist), Malcolm X (civil rights activist).

Entertainment

ELVIS PRESLEY (1935–1977)
Elvis Presley took America by storm in the mid-1950s with his wild pelvic gyrations, delighting teens and appalling parents across the country. Born and raised in Tupelo, Mississippi, Elvis was exposed to gospel music and began playing the guitar at an early age. He made his first recording in 1953, and skyrocketed to fame around 1956. He continued to dominate rock 'n' roll music well into the 1960s and remained a popular performer until his death in 1977. In addition to performing songs such as "Heartbreak Hotel," "Love Me Tender," and "Don't be Cruel," Elvis appeared in many movies. Graceland, Elvis's mansion in Memphis, Tennessee, has been turned into a multi-million dollar tourist attraction, and thousands of his fans gather there in January and August, on the anniversaries of his birth and death, to mourn.

MARILYN MONROE (1926–1962)
Born Norma Jeane Mortenson (she later took her mother's married name, Baker), Marilyn Monroe became a world-famous sex symbol and a Hollywood legend. Monroe was known for her seductive movie

roles and her breathy style of singing and speaking. Her personal life was as colorful as her onscreen performances, and she made headlines with her appearance in the debut issue of *Playboy*, with her marriages to baseball player Joe DiMaggio and playwright Arthur Miller, and with her alleged liaisons with both John and Robert Kennedy. Monroe overdosed on barbiturates at age 36. Some of her most well-known screen roles were in *The Seven-Year Itch, Some Like It Hot, Bus Stop,* and *The Misfits.*

Other important names: George and Ira Gershwin (composers), Cole Porter (composer), Frank Sinatra (singer and actor), Aretha Franklin (singer), Jimi Hendrix (musician), Bob Dylan (musician), Walt Disney (cartoonist).

Sports

GEORGE HERMAN "BABE" RUTH (1895–1948)

Babe Ruth played baseball for the Chicago Red Sox and the Boston Braves during his career, but he is best known as a New York Yankee. Ruth held the record for the most home runs in a season for 10 years, and in 1927, he set a record for most home runs (60) in a season. His record number of home runs (714) throughout his career was unbroken for almost 40 years. He led the Yankees to seven major league pennants (championships). Yankee Stadium, built for the New York Yankees in 1923, is still known as "The House that Ruth Built."

MUHAMMAD ALI (1942–)

Muhammad Ali's very public political battles contributed to his status as a sports icon as much as his flamboyant boxing style did. Born Cassius Clay, he adopted the name Muhammad Ali when he joined the Nation of Islam. In 1960, Ali won an Olympic gold medal in boxing, and in 1964, he became World Heavyweight Champion, a title he would defend nine times. In 1967, Ali refused to enter the armed services during the Vietnam War and was stripped of his title and barred from fighting until the U.S. Supreme Court upheld his draft appeal on religious grounds. At his retirement, Ali had a 56–5 record and was

the first man to ever win the heavyweight crown three times. Even in retirement, the boxer who "floats like a butterfly and stings like a bee" remains one of the sporting world's most recognized characters.

Other important names: Babe Didrikson (various sports, including golf and track and field), Bobby Fisher (chess), Michael Jordan (basketball), Billie Jean King (tennis), Joe Louis (boxing), Jesse Owens (track and field), Jackie Robinson (baseball), Secretariat (racehorse).

Arts and Literature

MARK TWAIN (1835–1910)

Mark Twain is the pen name of Samuel Langhorne Clemens, born in the backwoods of Missouri and raised on the banks of the Mississippi River. Twain had a passion for the mighty Mississippi River and eventually became a riverboat pilot after working many years as a printer and journalist. His pen name is derived from a nautical term meaning "two fathoms." Twain's writing was full of humor and social commentary and was often taken from events in his own life; his characters were frequently based on the people he knew. Many of Twain's stories are told through the eyes of children and young people; his most beloved characters are Tom Sawyer and Huckleberry Finn, the young duo that was constantly getting into trouble. Although he wrote countless articles and books, his best known are *The Adventures of Tom Sawyer*, *The Adventures of Huckleberry Finn*, and *Life on the Mississippi*.

ERNEST HEMINGWAY (1898–1961)

As a boy growing up in Illinois, Ernest Hemingway learned the values embodied in his writing, values such as courage and endurance. He was part of the "lost generation," a generation of Americans who experienced World War I and afterward felt alienated from their country. Hemingway often wrote about war and its impact on people, or about sports or contests that require stamina and courage, such as bullfighting. Hemingway's writing style was economical and understated, yet full of action. For Hemingway's characters, heroism lay not in some inborn talent, but in the constant struggle to conquer one's fear, especially one's fear of oneself. Like many of his characters, Hemingway himself was larger than life. He created for himself an almost mythological image of a soldier, fighter, and literary genius. His public persona as "Papa" Hemingway increasingly masked his private struggles with depression and paranoia, which eventually led to suicide. Some of his best-known works are *The Sun Also Rises*, *A Farewell to Arms*, *The Old Man and the Sea*, and *For Whom the Bell Tolls*.

Other important names: Ansel Adams (photographer), Dorthea Lange (photographer), Georgia O'Keeffe (painter), Edgar Allen Poe (writer), Harriet Beecher Stowe (writer), Henry David Thoreau (essayist and writer), Andy Warhol (artist), Frank Lloyd Wright (architect).

Inventors and Scientists

THOMAS ALVA EDISON (1847–1931)

Hailed as a genius in the practical application of science, Thomas Alva Edison was a prolific inventor. His first inventions were a transmitter and receiver for the automatic telegraph and a system for transmitting simultaneous telegraph messages. In 1877, he invented the microphone, and in 1878, he patented the first successful phonograph. Edison is credited with designing the first practical incandescent lamp and, along with it, a complete electrical distribution system for light and power. His experiments in the synchronization of moving pictures and sound were the basis for talking pictures. When all was said and done, Edison held more than 1,300 U.S. and foreign patents.

HENRY FORD (1863–1947)

An industrialist and pioneer in automobile manufacturing, Henry Ford completed his first automobile in 1896; three years later he launched the Detroit Automobile Company. In 1907, Ford and several partners organized the Ford Motor Company; he later purchased most of his partners' shares, giving the Ford family control of the company. Ford brought assembly line manufacturing to automobile production, cutting the costs of production and making automobiles more easily attainable. Ford soon outdistanced all competitors and became the largest automobile producer in the world, thanks to his implementation of mass production.

Other important names: Benjamin Franklin (scientist, inventor, printer, statesman, and philosopher), Robert Fulton (inventor), Samuel Morse (inventor), Sally Ride (astronaut), Jonas Salk (scientist), Orville and Wilbur Wright (inventors and aviators).

POLITICS & GOVERNMENT

The Government System

The United States consists of 49 states and 1 district. The latter, Washington, D.C., is the capital of the United States. State government plays an important role in politics; many policy, administrative, and regulatory decisions are made at the state level.

The 50 States

STATE	CAPITAL	ABBREVIATION*
Alabama	Montgomery	AL
Alaska	Juneau	AK
Arizona	Phoenix	AZ
Arkansas	Little Rock	AR
California	Sacramento	CA
Colorado	Denver	CO
Connecticut	Hartford	CT
Delaware	Dover	DE
Florida	Tallahassee	FL
Georgia	Atlanta	GA
Hawaii	Honolulu	HI
Idaho	Boise	ID
Illinois	Springfield	IL
Indiana	Indianapolis	IN
Iowa	Des Moines	IA
Kansas	Topeka	KS
Kentucky	Frankfort	KY
Louisiana	Baton Rouge	LA
Maine	Augusta	ME
Maryland	Annapolis	MD
Massachusetts	Boston	MA
Michigan	Lansing	MI
Minnesota	St. Paul	MN
Mississippi	Jackson	MS
Missouri	Jefferson City	MO
Montana	Helena	MT
Nebraska	Lincoln	NE
Nevada	Carson City	NV

* These abbreviations are used in many different situations, although you will see them most often in addresses.

New Hampshire	Concord	NH
New Jersey	Trenton	NJ
New Mexico	Santa Fe	NM
New York	Albany	NY
North Carolina	Raleigh	NC
North Dakota	Bismarck	ND
Ohio	Columbus	OH
Oklahoma	Oklahoma City	OK
Oregon	Salem	OR
Pennsylvania	Harrisburg	PA
Rhode Island	Providence	RI
South Carolina	Columbia	SC
South Dakota	Pierre	SD
Tennessee	Nashville	TN
Texas	Austin	TX
Utah	Salt Lake City	UT
Vermont	Montpelier	VT
Virginia	Richmond	VA
Washington	Olympia	WA
West Virginia	Charleston	WV
Wisconsin	Madison	WI
Wyoming	Cheyenne	WY

The United States also has the following dependent areas: American Samoa, Baker Island, Guam, Howland Island, Jarvis Island, Johnston Atoll, Kingman Reef, Midway Islands, Navassa Island, Northern Mariana Islands, Palmyra Atoll, Puerto Rico, Virgin Islands, and Wake Island.

The Executive Branch

The chief of state and head of government is the president. The president and vice president run for office on the same ballot and are therefore elected together. Both serve four-year terms and can be elected to a second term in office.

Cabinet members, who assist the president in administering the government, are appointed by the president but require approval by the Senate (see "Legislative Branch"). There are 14 cabinet positions: the U.S. Attorney General and the Secretaries of the Departments of State, Treasury, Defense, Interior, Agriculture, Commerce, Labor, Health and Human Services, Education, Housing and Urban Development, Transportation, Energy, and Veterans' Affairs.

Election of the president and vice president is done on two levels. Each registered voter casts his or her individual vote. All Americans are eligible to register to vote at age 18. However, because the United States has an electoral college system, there is a second level of vote. Each state has a designated number of electors and electoral votes based on the number of representatives the state has in Congress (based on the state's population). The process of nominating electors varies from state to state, but voters in each state select the nominees during the general election in November. The electors then meet in December to cast their votes for the president and vice president. The presidency and vice presidency are won by electoral vote, not by the votes cast by the American voters. While the electors are not legally bound to cast their votes according to the results of the popular vote in their states, it is very rare for them to vote otherwise. Forty-eight states adopt a winner-takes-all stance when it comes to their electoral votes. That is, the candidate who wins the popular votes in the state gets all of the state's electoral votes. Only in Maine and Nebraska can the electoral votes be divided between candidates.

Under the U.S. Constitution, it is the electoral vote that counts. This electoral college system means that it is possible for a candidate to win the nationwide popular vote but lose the presidency according to the electoral vote. The electoral college system of voting has come under fire recently for this reason. A combination of issues and events has recently caused Americans to take a long, hard look at their system. Very few elections have resulted in a presidency awarded to a candidate who won the electoral vote but did not win the popular vote. Several candidates have won based on very narrow margins.

The system has evolved since its beginnings, when state legislatures cast electoral votes without a statewide popular vote, and amendments to the Constitution have helped it change with the times. Many people, however, feel that the U.S. government should be a government "for the people, by the people," as it states in the Constitution. There is a growing sentiment that the electoral college system is outdated, especially since technology seems to make it possible to truly elect by popular vote. Other proposals have been made to select electors by district rather than by state, or to keep the electoral college system but eliminate the electors as individuals. However, any change to the way Americans vote will require an amendment to the Constitution.

The Legislative Branch

The legislative branch of the U.S. government consists of the Senate and the House of Representatives; together, these are referred to as Congress. There are 100 Senate seats; each state elects two Senators. Senators serve for six years, but to maintain continuity, elections are staggered so that one-third of the Senate is newly elected every two years. There are 435 seats in the House of Representatives, whose members are elected by direct popular vote. The number of representatives elected by each state varies according to population, but all serve two-year terms.

The Judicial Branch

The judicial branch is the Supreme Court, which oversees a system of federal courts. There are nine Supreme Court justices. These justices are appointed for life by the president, with confirmation by the Senate.

Political Parties

Following America's independence, people had different ideas about the course that the newly independent country should follow. This division led to the formation of two political parties. Since that time, the United States has had two major political parties, although the names and issues have changed. In addition, there are several smaller parties that have played an increasing role in American politics. However, most publicly elected offices are filled by a system that gives the post to the individual who receives the most votes. There is no proportioning system where each party is allocated a certain number of seats or where any party that receives a specified percentage of votes gains seats. The American system propagates the two-party system and makes it difficult for candidates from smaller parties to get elected.

Voters can register as members of any established party, or they can choose to remain independent. Party members are eligible to vote in all party or primary elections, such as the selection of the party's presidential candidate. People who registered with no party affiliation cannot vote in any party's internal election, but can participate in all general elections, such as gubernatorial and presidential elections. Voters can vote for any candidate on the ballot in general elections; they are not obligated to vote for their party's candidate, although they often do.

The nature of both parties and their candidates varies from area to area, and not every member of a political party thinks the same. However, in general, the Republican Party is considered to be more conservative than the Democratic Party and very much influenced by business and industry. Democrats are considered more liberal. Labor associations, urban organizations, and ethnic minority groups tend to be more allied with the Democratic Party than with the Republican Party.

REPUBLICAN PARTY

Like the Democratic Party, the Republican Party has its roots in the early Federalist party, formed in the late 1700s. Federalists advocated a strong, centralized government that would support the interests of commerce and industry. This was replaced in 1828 by the Whigs, a large number of whom had split from the Democratic Party. The Whigs, in turn, were replaced by the Republican Party in 1854. At that time, the United States was on the cusp of the Civil War, and the Republican Party called for an end to slavery in all territories.

Of course, different politicians and local party affiliates have different agendas. However, two examples of common Republican Party ideals are the belief that the United States must continue to build and maintain its military strength, and that power needs to be shifted from the federal government to the state and local governments.

DEMOCRATIC PARTY

The Democratic Party is the oldest continuous political party in the United States, and it has historically dominated the political landscape. Its evolution can be traced back to the late 1700s and the Democratic-Republicans, who favored a decentralized republic with limited power given to the federal government. Landmark events, such as the election of John Quincy Adams in 1824 and the policy regarding slavery (some supported an anti-slavery policy, while others felt that each territory should decide on its own whether or not to abolish slavery), led to splintering of the Party, but the foundations remained strong. In 1844, the party was officially renamed the Democratic Party.

Issues that are important to most Democrats are moving toward a less bureaucratic government, preserving social programs such as Medicare and Social Security, and protecting the environment.

ECONOMY

The United States has a dynamic market-based economy with many industries on the leading edge of technological advances. The U.S. economy is the largest in the world and is twice that of Japan, the second largest. The American standard of living is among the highest in the world.

Although the government does not hold any interest in private business, it does play an important role in the economy, setting the standards for regulation in some industries and ensuring that economic opportunities are accessible to everyone. Businesses and special interest groups, in turn, often lobby government officials to ensure that their interests are considered when government policy decisions are made. The government itself buys many goods and services from private companies.

The American approach to international trade is predominantly pro–free trade, although this was not always the case. Prior to World War II, the U.S. international trade policies included high tariffs. This isolationism, however, helped contribute to the Great Depression in the 1930s, and following World War II, policies were modified to encourage more free trade. Expanding the horizons of international trade has had its problems, however. U.S. firms find that while their foreign competitors have relatively easy access to the U.S. market, they don't always have the same access to the foreign markets, making it more difficult to compete.

Particularly challenging issues for the U.S. economy are the rising costs of providing for an aging population and a widening gap in skills in the labor market. The U.S. government provides retired people with an income through the Social Security program and with subsidized medical care through programs such as Medicare and Medicaid. However, these systems are funded through taxing the income of working Americans, and forecasts are grim. Due to changing population patterns and other factors, Social Security funds will probably run out in the foreseeable future. Various proposals have been put forth, both as alternatives to Social Security and to increase the funds available. One example of the latter is to invest Social Security funds in the stock market, a plan that many find untenable because of the unstable nature of the market, likening it to gambling away the country's savings.

The labor market in the United States is one of the most highly educated and skilled in the world. However, due to the rapid advancement in technology, there is a large gap between the most and least skilled. While approximately 80% of jobs are in service, gains in income go to those who are already in the upper earning tiers, and the incomes of those in lower economic tiers remain stagnant.

HOLIDAYS & CELEBRATIONS

The United States does not actually have any public holidays mandated by the government. Each state, and, indeed, each company may choose to recognize holidays or not. Most places elect to follow the lead of the federal government and observe those same holidays, which are listed below. In addition, some states or cities observe local holidays.

January 1	New Year's Day
3rd Monday in January	Martin Luther King Jr. Day
3rd Monday in February	Presidents' Day
4th Monday in May	Memorial Day
July 4	Independence Day (Fourth of July)
1st Monday of September	Labor Day
2nd Monday in October	Columbus Day
November 11	Veterans Day
4th Thursday in November	Thanksgiving
December 25	Christmas

Let's take a closer look at some of these holidays, as well as some other important celebrations.

New Year's Day

Like much of the rest of the world, Americans celebrate the beginning of a new year on January 1st. The festivities begin on December 31, New Year's Eve, with champagne at parties ranging from a small gathering of friends and family to large, formal balls. (Many people get at least a half a day off from work on December 31.) After counting down the final seconds to the new year, couples exchange kisses and people sing (or hum—most people only know the first few words!) "Auld Lang Syne," a song about old times fondly remembered.

Martin Luther King Jr. Day

This day is America's newest holiday. In 1973, Illinois instituted Martin Luther King Jr. Day as a state holiday; it became a federal holiday in 1983, the result of persistent lobbying in the 15 years since King's assassination. A number of states resisted recognizing the day as a state holiday, but in 1999, New Hampshire became the last of the 50 states to adopt the day as a state holiday. Although King was born on January 15th, the holiday is observed on the 3rd Monday in January. This holiday celebrates the life and leadership of the civil rights leader. Many people consider the day to be one of service, not just a day off work, and they use the time to volunteer or participate in marches to promote King's memory and the need to continue on the path toward fully realized civil rights and racial equality. In some Southern states, this holiday is ironically combined with the birthday of Robert E. Lee, the leader of the Confederate Army during the Civil War.

Valentine's Day (February 14)

Named after an early Christian martyr, Valentine's Day in America has become a thoroughly commercialized day of public and private affection. Couples exchange cards and gifts (chocolates and roses are popular) as a token of love. Children may receive candy or gifts from their parents, or they may exchange cards with their classmates at school. Although Valentine's Day is heavily promoted in stores, people do not get a day off from work.

Presidents' Day

Until the mid-1970s, Americans celebrated the birthdays of two presidents: George Washington, on February 22, was a federal holiday, and Abraham Lincoln, on February 12, was a holiday in most states. In the majority of states, the days have been combined and the celebration has been expanded to embrace all past presidents. A few states continue to recognize Lincoln's birthday as a separate holiday.

St. Patrick's Day (March 17)

Although St. Patrick's Day is really an Irish celebration, the whole country is "Irish" on March 17! Many American communities have a parade to celebrate the day, and many people, Irish or not, wear at least a little green. In some communities, corned beef and cabbage is the traditional meal for the day, and beer drinking (often green-colored beer) becomes the national pastime, if only for one night.

Good Friday and Easter

Good Friday and Easter fall on the first Friday and Sunday after the first full moon on, or following, the spring equinox (March 21), a complicated formula that most Americans are not familiar with—they simply look at the list of holidays printed on their calendars to see when Good Friday and Easter will be each year. These holidays commemorate the Christian belief in the crucifixion and subsequent resurrection of Jesus Christ. For Christians, Easter is a day of religious services and the gathering of family. Many Americans follow the tradition of coloring hard-boiled eggs, which the adults often hide around the house or yard for the children to find, and giving children baskets of candy, said to have been brought by the Easter Bunny. The day after Easter Sunday, Easter Monday, the president of the United States holds an annual Easter egg hunt on the White House lawn for young children.

Mother's Day (2nd Sunday in May)

All mothers are celebrated on this family-oriented holiday. Mothers receive cards and gifts from their children, grandchildren, and husbands. Some families have their own traditions, such as serving Mom breakfast in bed or going to a restaurant for a special dinner.

Administrative Professionals Week

This "holiday" began as Secretary's Day, one day set aside for the appreciation of secretaries, typists, and stenographers. It has grown into a week-long observance in April, renamed Administrative Professionals Week. As a casual observer, you may not notice much difference in the workplace. However, most people do recognize the contributions of their support staff in some way, large or small. You can find more information in the "Gift-Giving" section of the "Living and Staying in the United States" chapter.

Memorial Day

Memorial Day began as Decoration Day, established in 1868 as a day to decorate the graves of those who died in the Civil War. Following World War I, it was renamed Memorial Day, and now honors all Americans who gave their lives in battle. Many cities have parades to celebrate Memorial Day, and many people fly the American flag at their homes on this day as a sign of respect.

Father's Day (3rd Sunday in June)

Like Mother's Day, Father's Day is a family celebration. Cards and gifts are given by family members, and other family traditions are observed.

Independence Day

The Declaration of Independence (from England) was signed on July 4, 1776, America's "birthday." More commonly called the Fourth of July, this is a day of patriotic parades, picnics, and concerts, all topped off with dazzling displays of fireworks. When this day falls on a weekend, most people get the preceding Friday or following Monday off from work.

Labor Day

Labor Day honors the country's working people. Some communities have parades or events. In many places, Labor Day marks the end of summer vacation for students and the beginning of the school year.

Columbus Day

Columbus Day commemorates October 12, 1492, the day the Italian explorer Christopher Columbus landed in the New World. In some communities, parades and other events mark this day.

Halloween (October 31)

Halloween is a uniquely American holiday. The origins of Halloween are in All Hallows' Eve, the day before All Saint's Day. (*Hallow* is the Old English word for "saint.") Many of the customs surrounding this time predate Christianity and have their roots in Celtic beliefs. It was thought that witches and other evil spirits came out on the evening before All Saint's Day, playing tricks on humans. Bonfires were made to ward off this evil, and offerings of foods and sweets were made to the spirits. People disguised themselves as spirits in an attempt to avoid detection by the evil ones. Today, Halloween is a popular holiday with children, who dress up in costumes and go door-to-door throughout their neighborhoods, ringing doorbells and saying "Trick or Treat." You are expected to give them "treats" (usually candy) so that they won't play a "trick" on you. If there are children in your neighborhood, be sure to stock up on candy before October 31! Haunted houses, houses decorated with gruesome images to horrify and thrill those who enter, are popular; some people decorate their homes with carved pumpkins and other Halloween themes. Adults and children alike often attend costume parties.

Veterans Day

Veterans Day began as Armistice Day, the day that marks the end of World War I, November 11, 1918. It was established to honor Americans who served in the war. Today, Veterans Day honors the veterans of all wars in which America fought. Veterans' organizations have parades and memorial services, and the president places a memorial wreath on the Tomb of the Unknowns (a memorial to the unknown soldiers who died in battle) at Arlington National Cemetery in Washington, D.C.

Thanksgiving

Thanksgiving dates back to 1621, when the Puritan Pilgrims arrived in Massachusetts, fleeing from religious persecution in England. Their first year in the New World was difficult, and many died during the rough winter. In the spring, they sought help from neighboring Native Americans, who taught them how to plant corn and other crops. At the fall harvest, the Pilgrims gave thanks by holding a feast, which became a national tradition. Today, Thanksgiving is a day when families gather together to give thanks for the bounty in their own lives. A typical Thanksgiving dinner table bursts with roast turkey, cranberry sauce, and pumpkin pie, among other things. School children often participate in a play that reenacts the story of the Pilgrims and the Native Americans. Because the holiday always falls on a Thursday, many people take the following Friday off from work so they can have a four-day weekend.

Christmas

Christmas is a Christian holiday celebrating the birth of Jesus Christ. On Christmas or Christmas Eve (December 24), Christians, Catholic or Protestant, attend church services. In the United States, Christmas has become quite commercialized, and the giving of gifts has gradually overshadowed the religious origins of the holiday. Christmas is a family holiday, and each family has its own traditions. Many families put up and decorate fir or pine Christmas trees, often weeks before Christmas, and exchange Christmas gifts. You will also see many homes decorated with lights and other ornaments, some very elaborately.

Many American kids believe in Santa Claus—a red-suited, bearded, jolly old fellow—who works year-round with his elves at the North Pole to fulfill the Christmas wishes of children. He visits children on Christmas Eve, stuffing the stockings they have left out for him. Children who have been good receive toys, while bad children receive coal—although the coal is more of a threat by parents to get their kids to behave. Children often leave milk and cookies for Santa and the nine reindeer that pull his sleigh.

Other Important Holidays and Local Events

In addition to these holidays, you will find that other celebrations take place on a local level. For example, Mardi Gras is a time of wild celebration in New Orleans, Louisiana. Marking the beginning of Lent, a Catholic penitential season, the citizens of New Orleans—and throngs of visitors—have parades and generally revel in excess for several days.

Other groups observe special days as well. Jewish Americans observe the high holy days of Yom Kippur and Rosh Hashanah in the fall as well as other holidays, such as Passover and Hanukkah. Many Mexican-American communities, especially in southern California, celebrate Cinco de Mayo (May 5). For many African Americans, Kwanzaa, celebrated from December 26 to January 1, is a way of connecting to their African cultural identity. If you are interested in participating in your community's special holidays, you can find information on dates and events in the local newspaper.

EDUCATION

Primary and Secondary Education

The United States does not have a national school system; each state regulates its own schools. Local and state taxes, along with some funding from the federal government, fund schools. Since policies and standards are set by each state, school systems vary. The first school level is elementary school, beginning with kindergarten. Children usually start kindergarten at age four or five. Elementary school can last through the 8th grade, followed by secondary school—called high school—from grades nine to twelve. However, in many schools, elementary school ends after the 6th grade and is followed by middle school, or junior high school, from grades seven through nine, with high school beginning at grade ten.

School attendance is mandatory for children, but in most states, a child might voluntarily leave school at the age of 16. Subject matter can vary from state to state, but many classes are taught virtually everywhere, such as mathematics, science, English (reading, grammar, writing, and literature), social studies (history, geography, civics), and physical education. Most schools offer both required and elective courses, such as foreign languages, driver's education, home economics (also known as home and careers), and shop (sometimes called industrial technology, where students learn about the use of tools and the basics of carpentry, machinery, etc.).

While 90% of American children attend public school (there is no tuition), parents can also choose to send their children to private schools, which do charge tuition. About 80% of these private schools are run by religious groups, and religious instruction is part of the curriculum. Home schooling is also an option for parents who wish to educate their children themselves.

Higher Education

Following graduation from high school, students have several choices for continuing their education, either through continued academic studies or vocational training. Higher education is not free, although it is possible for students to get financial aid through scholarships, grants, and loans. Generally speaking, private colleges and universities cost more than their state-run counterparts. Additionally, students who attend a state-run college or university in the state where they live are charged less than those who attend from out of state.

Quality programs can be found in both state and private institutions. However, some schools have more prestige, especially those known as Ivy League schools, eight high-status schools in the Northeast (Brown, Columbia, Cornell, Dartmouth, Harvard, Princeton, University of Pennsylvania, and Yale). Places in these well-regarded schools are coveted, since graduates are generally able to find employment easily when they graduate from these schools.

A college offers a four-year course of study that leads to a Bachelor of Arts (BA) or Bachelor of Science (BS) degree. A university is a larger institution that offers advanced Master's and PhD (Doctor of Philosophy) degrees in addition to Bachelor's degrees. However, this distinction between colleges and universities has begun to blur.

In a typical four-year program, a student will spend two years taking required courses in a variety of subjects, followed by two years of specialization in their major field of study. Many students, especially those pursuing liberal arts degrees, enter college with no real idea of what major they want to pursue; in fact, it's not uncommon for students to switch majors one or more times before finally settling on a field of study.

Students often enter the work world right after receiving their Bachelor's degree. Some, however, choose to continue on to get a Master's degree or even a PhD, or follow a specialized course of study, such as medicine, law, or seminary (religious studies for those who wish to enter the ministry). These advanced degrees require additional studies of one year to eight or more years, depending on the course of study chosen.

Community and junior colleges provide an option for students who want to approach college more slowly or receive a degree in only two years. They can also be a cost-efficient way to receive college credit before transferring to a larger, more expensive college or university. Students often continue to live at home while they attend a nearby community or junior college.

About 25% of colleges and universities are privately run by religious groups, although they are open to students of all faiths. These institutions usually require that students take classes on religion studies in addition to their regular studies.

For young adults who want to learn a vocation instead of pursuing academics, vocational schools offer courses for people who are interested in learning the skills necessary to become electricians, plumbers, mechanics, medical and legal assistants, cosmeticians, etc.

IMPORTANT ISSUES

Violence

It seems that violence is in the news almost every day in America. This appears in many forms: domestic, child, or spousal abuse; racial violence and bias crimes, such as crimes victimizing homosexuals;

gang violence. Even "road rage" (fits of anger by motorists, some-times violent, directed at pedestrians or other motorists) has become common. Disturbing trends have surfaced in violence in schools and in the workplace.

Some people blame increases in violence on television, movies, video and computer games, and music. Indeed, the American enter-tainment industry is more comfortable with violence than it is with sex; violence in movies and on television is commonplace, while sex is more censored.

Some people, however, place more blame on easy access to weapons. In fact, one of the most hotly debated issues in America today is gun control. Proponents of gun control would like to see more regulation of gun ownership, if not outright abolishment. Gun owners, led by the NRA (National Rifle Association), defend their right to "bear arms," as outlined in the Constitution.

Drug Control

The United States has been waging war on drugs for decades. Cur-rent governmental policy seeks to prevent young people from start-ing to use drugs by imposing stiff penalties for those who import and sell drugs. Recently, the government has allied with the governments of Columbia and other countries that export drugs to work toward the common goal of eradicating illegal drug trafficking.

Peripheral to this issue is the question of drug legalization. Dif-ferent groups advocate different policy changes; some advocate le-galizing all drugs or legalizing and regulating only certain drugs, such as those that have medicinal uses, like marijuana. All in all, however, there is still a strong consensus in America that drugs should remain illegal, though many do sympathize with the use of drugs for medical reasons.

There is also a growing problem of drug abuse in the United States. Statistics from the Office of National Drug Control Policy in-dicate that some 14.8 million Americans 12 years of age and older, about 6.7% of the population, are drug users. While this figure is gradually decreasing, the problem is far from being solved.

Health Care

The issue of health care has recently come into the spotlight in the United States, as its costs have risen astronomically, and Americans are feeling the pinch in their wallets. Health care is a private industry, although the government does have programs in place to provide assistance to the poor and the elderly. Most people, however, rely on health insurance to pay for their health care. Over the past decades, much of the health-care system has been consolidated into managed organizations. However, because these health-care management organizations are in business to make a profit, there is some concern that the quality of health care and the well-being of patients are being sacrificed for profits.

CULTURE

We all have programmed in us a certain code, a set of rules by which we live and interpret the world. These rules govern both our actions and our reactions. They are instilled in us by our parents, our teachers, and our peers. Culture, then, is the combined values, beliefs, mores, motivations, and attitudes that shape our view of the world.

Although we are all individuals, we are all influenced by the culture in which we grew up. Despite our individual differences, there are nevertheless cultural ties that bind us together. You are probably quite conscious of cultural differences within your own country, but in fact, most people have more in common with people from their own country than they do with someone from halfway around the globe.

This chapter explores the culture of the United States and compares it to other cultures around the world. Although endless distinctions can be made between cultures, here we break down culture into six different categories that will paint a practical, accessible portrait of American culture. These categories are: time, communication, group dynamics, status & hierarchy, relationships, and reasoning. Each section begins with a brief overview of the category and the polar opposites within it. As we explore the category in more depth, we will take a look at where the United States falls on the continuum and how that can differ from other cultures. By the end of the section, you should have a greater understanding of what might cause cultural misunderstanding and an idea of the very real challenges communicating across cultures can present. Finally, we will provide you with some tips to help you apply this information to your daily interactions with Americans. We will use this knowledge as we take a step-by-step look at the American business culture in later chapters.

With any luck, you will emerge with a better understanding not only of what makes Americans tick, but of what makes *you* tick, as well. Only when you are able to understand that cultural differences are neither bad nor good, merely different ways to look at the same reality, can you begin to build the cross-cultural skills you will need to be successful in the United States—or anywhere else in the world.

The following observations contain generalizations out of necessity. It is naturally unwise to think that every American will behave in one way. However, there is enough evidence to support the idea that Americans as a culture tend to have certain preferences, as do the peoples of other countries. Keeping that in mind, the information in this chapter will give you a foundation on which to lay the bricks of individual characteristics and personalities.

TIME

Luiz Camargo, the sales manager for the South American region of an international tool manufacturing company, was finding it more

and more difficult to work with Gina Hilton, the company's American manager of human resources. Gina had met with Luiz several months ago to outline her plan for reconfigurating both the compensation structure for sales representatives and the annual reviews process. According to Gina's plan, the new procedures were to be fully implemented within six months. Several incidents occurred that made it impossible for Luiz to meet the proposed deadlines, but he was not concerned. In the end things would work out, and, after all, wasn't the goal itself more important than the date? Gina, however, seemed to feel that he was deliberately stalling, and she sent e-mails and called almost weekly to remind him of the importance of the project, pushing him to meet deadlines. Luiz began to feel more and more harassed by Gina, but the last straw was when Gina made another trip to Brazil and met with Luiz's vice president to complain about Luiz's so-called "lack of cooperation."

Although interpersonal problems are always a possibility whenever two or more people are involved, it is most likely that the problems that arose in the scenario above are the result of different views of time.

Rigid versus Flexible Cultures

Perhaps the first cultural challenge people encounter when they meet another culture is the difference in perception of time. Time is a resource that different cultures view in different ways. We all have varied answers to the questions What is the value of time? and How is time best spent? In the most basic terms, time can be either flexible or rigid.

In a rigid-time culture, the clock is the measure against which all of our actions are judged: whether we are saving time or wasting it, whether we are on time or late. People in rigid-time cultures like to plan their activities and keep a schedule. It is rude to show up late and important not to waste other people's time. Time is a commodity that must be spent wisely, not squandered.

The clock for flexible-time cultures is more fluid, and things can happen more spontaneously. Plans are made with the understanding that they may be changed, even at the last minute, depending on circumstances. Punctuality is not a virtue, and many things can take precedence over adherence to a schedule.

Interacting with Americans

The United States falls on the rigid end of the time spectrum, although there are some cultures that are more time conscious. For example, Germans have the reputation of being one of the most, if not the most, time-conscious cultures in the world. Cultures that have more flexible views of time are Mexico, China, Italy, Egypt, and Saudi Arabia.

The United States and Flexible-Time Cultures

Americans in general find themselves ruled by the clock. Time is a limited asset that Americans schedule carefully and often fully. The American business person's accessories are incomplete without an ever-present daily planner, which is divided into half-hour or even 15-minute increments in order to allow close scheduling. Sometimes the planner is computerized, either on a desktop computer or a Personal Digital Assistant, with automatic reminders of the time and date of an appointment. With such tight scheduling, people inevitably run late, but extreme or frequent tardiness is discourteous and will, at best, irritate the people whom you have inconvenienced.

Americans do like their schedules, but these schedules are flexible in the sense that last-minute appointments and cancellations are accepted. American business people, especially those in management positions, are expected to meet deadlines and finish projects, even if it means staying until the early hours of the morning. By the same token, in China, a missed or delayed deadline (which is, after all, only a target) is neither a crisis nor a reason to panic. It is merely a change in plans, and, as past experience has shown, all will most likely work out in the end.

People from flexible-time cultures tend to have a much more relaxed approach to time. Appointments and schedules act more as guidelines, and it's understood that other things are more important than paying obeisance to the clock. If, for instance, a Brazilian is speaking with a colleague in his office, he won't cut him short or rush him off simply because it is time for another appointment. An American in the same situation would probably prefer to schedule another meeting with his colleague to continue the discussion at a later date so that he can keep his scheduled appointment.

The United States and Rigid-Time Cultures

Although the United States is itself a rigid-time culture, American time consciousness is all about speed rather than efficiency. People from cultures whose time consciousness comes in the form of careful planning and efficiency often feel that Americans waste a lot of time "at the coffee machine"; that is, they spend too much time chatting with their coworkers instead of doing their jobs. If Americans were only more efficient, think the Germans, they wouldn't have to stay until 7:00 every night just to get their jobs done. Americans, on the other hand, are astonished when the Germans pick up and leave promptly at 5:00. This, they think, must mean that the Germans don't have the same amount of dedication to their jobs, when, in fact, it is indicative of the importance Germans place on the efficient use of time.

Tips on Time

- Be on time! This applies to both business appointments and social occasions, although there is a limited window of acceptable tardiness for social events (see the section titled "Be My Guest: Being on Your Best Behavior as a Host or Guest" in the "Living and Staying in the United States" chapter).
- Try to plan ahead as much as possible. Americans usually prefer to have several days' notice for both business appointments and social gatherings, although last-minute requests are occasionally acceptable.
- Americans tend to overbook, which can cause them to run late for meetings and appointments, making it necessary for them to leave even if there is more to be discussed. Be prepared to schedule a follow-up meeting or phone call rather than extending the meeting's end time.
- Americans often schedule appointments by saying they will "pencil you in." The "pencil" part of the phrase means that if something more important comes up, you will get rescheduled. It helps to reconfirm appointments before showing up for them.
- Remember that as a rule most Americans prefer that you make arrangements to meet, rather than just dropping by their homes without warning. This applies even if your friend says, "You'll have to stop by sometime."

COMMUNICATION

Sabine Bergmann left her boss's office feeling very confused. Her meeting with her boss had been part of her annual review. Her boss had started by complimenting her on things that she considered to be just part of her job: being on time to work and completing tasks in a timely fashion. Then her boss went on to say that Sabine needed to improve her working relationships with her coworkers, who often found her to be aloof and unfriendly.

Direct versus Indirect Communication

What is the goal of communication? Regardless of what culture you are from, you need to be able to relay information to other people. But is that the goal in and of itself, or are there other variables that affect the goal?

In cultures that value direct communication, the goal of communication is mainly to relay information. Value is placed on being able to state your point in a clear and concise manner, and words have limited nuances. In general, people do not appreciate having to search for the real meaning among excess words.

If you live in a culture of indirect communication, on the other hand, you have to take other factors into account. It may be important to not cause offense to your listener, to show deference, or to maintain harmony, for example. Very often the real meaning in indirect-communication cultures is a subtext buried under many layers of meaning or intertwined with non-verbal clues or metaphor.

Interacting with Americans

Americans have many sayings about speaking directly. "Don't beat around the bush." "Just spit it out." "Get to the point." However, Americans also tend to lessen the damage of negative comments by framing them in a positive light. Therefore, if an American disagrees with an idea you have offered, he or she might say "That's an interesting idea, but . . ." and go on to tell you why it won't work. By doing this, Americans feel that they are sparing your feelings and encouraging you to continue to provide input before openly disagreeing with you.

As you can imagine, the American style of communication lies on the direct side of the continuum. However, just like in the time category, the United States is not the most direct culture. Australia, Germany, the Netherlands, and Israel are examples of countries that have more direct communication styles than the United States, while Japan, France, Kuwait, and Argentina are countries whose communication style is more indirect, to varying degrees.

The United States and Indirect-Communication Cultures

Americans place value on direct communication because it helps to get things done quickly. They are often impatient with someone who speaks indirectly or who approaches a problem obliquely, and may consider that person to be timid or think that he or she is hiding something. This is especially true when Americans feel they can't get a direct answer from someone.

For example, an American who asks a supplier if he will be able to meet the production deadline wants to hear a definitive answer. If the answer is "Yes, we will meet the deadline," the American expects the product to arrive by the deadline. If the answer is "No, we will not meet the deadline because . . .," the American can either adjust her own schedule or find a supplier who can meet the deadline. If the supplier in this scenario is from an indirect-communication culture, he may not want to say, "No" outright for various reasons and may be evasive by saying something like, "It is possible," or "I will try." The American may press for a more definite answer, forcing the supplier to say yes even though he knows it is not possible, or she may hear the indefinite response as a positive, and she is likely to be angry when the product does not arrive by the deadline.

People coming from cultures where indirect communication is the norm often feel that Americans are too frank and too pushy. The American tendency to speak in a direct fashion to superiors as well as to peers and subordinates strikes some indirect communicators as disrespectful.

The United States and Direct-Communication Cultures

On the other side of the communication equation are those cultures whose communication style is more direct than that of Americans. For example, Germans are very direct communicators, and they apply their communication style more universally than Americans.

One of the most common miscommunications that happens between Americans and their more direct counterparts is in the use of niceties, not only in social situations but in business as well. American workers are used to hearing "Could you do this?" "I need you to do this," and even "Would you mind doing that?" "Please" and "thank you" are standards of the American business vocabulary. Germans, for example, have a more implicit understanding of what one's duties are; therefore, it is not necessary for a boss to couch a directive as a request.

An American giving a performance review will start first with some positive comments: improvements that the employee has made, goals achieved, etc. This affirmation of the employee's contributions is followed by "constructive criticism," wherein the manager discusses goals not achieved, slippage in performance, and so on. Even here, the language is somewhat indirect, and directives for improvement are stated as suggestions for what could be done better. A German performance review would focus more on the improvements needed than the successes of the past year. Affirmation is not necessary, since it is expected that each person do his or her job. No news is assumed to be good news. When the two styles meet, you get either a German who feels confused and somewhat dazed by the back-and-forth of compliment and criticism or an American who feels personally assaulted and frustrated that his contributions weren't appreciated or even acknowledged.

Tips on Communicating

- If you are an indirect communicator, you will need to develop a thick skin. Remind yourself not to take it personally when you encounter the more direct style of speaking that is typical in the United States.
- Try to speak honestly and frankly, but don't confuse a direct communication style with rudeness; there is a difference between being frank and being tactless.
- Remember that Americans would rather hear the bad news immediately and directly so that they can change their plans or fix the problem. If you won't be able to meet a deadline, say so and explain why.
- Balance the negative with a positive. A common American lead-in is, "There's good news and there's bad news." The speaker may then go on to say that the good news is that sales are up and the bad news is that the sales manager quit.

- When dealing with other people's performance or ideas, preface negative comments with positive ones to ensure good morale.

GROUP DYNAMICS

Kazushi Yamaguchi had been working at an American company for about a month when his boss, Janice Richards, asked him to come into her office. Janice told him that she was disappointed with his lack of participation in their weekly team meetings. Very often, Janice asked her team to just toss out ideas on how they could improve any aspect of their work: work flow, communication, customer service, response time, etc. Janice used these brainstorming sessions as a way to stimulate ideas and creativity. She had noticed, however, that Kazushi never offered an idea for discussion and did not participate much in the discussion of others' ideas. In order to be an effective member of the team, she told him, he would need to show more willingness to contribute to their brainstorming sessions.

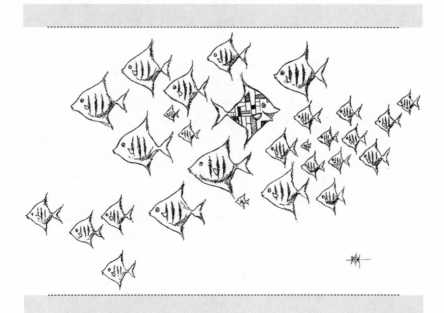

Group-Oriented Versus Individualistic

In the overall scheme of things, which is stronger: the needs of the individual or the needs of the group? Is it usually the case that individuals are willing to make sacrifices for the good of the group, or will the group suffer for the benefit of the individual?

At one time or another, we are all faced with making a decision to place someone else's needs before our own—our family, our friends, our team at work. Where the deeper cultural differences lie, however, is in the expectations of society. What is the societal norm for looking out for oneself or one's group? The next time you stay late at the office, think about your motives for doing so. Are you really staying to finish the project because it will be an enormous benefit to your company? Or are you staying because in order to advance up the ladder of success, it is important that you be perceived as dedicated and hard-working?

Groups can take on many forms. Your group might consist of your family (immediate or extended), coworkers, the company you work for, friends with whom you grew up and went to school, a tribe or a religious group, or a local, regional, or national affiliation. And of course you may belong to many different groups throughout your life.

If you are group-oriented, the group is an inherent part of your identity. You are first and foremost Japanese or a Muslim or Bantu or a member of the Fuentes family, and a major factor in your decisions and actions is how they affect other members of your group. As an individual, you are much more inclined to align your own goals with that of the group. Your talent is part of a larger pool, and when you cooperate with others, it becomes possible to reach a mutual goal.

For example, some of the sales people in your division brought in more revenue and some brought in less. However, the important thing is that the sales goals were met, so everyone should share equally in the annual bonus. In this way, individual weaknesses are compensated for by others' strengths so that a balance is achieved. The success of the team will strengthen it and encourage people to strive for higher goals.

The sales scenario wherein everyone shares equally in the bonus when some people have brought in more business than others seems unfair in individualistic cultures. A member of such a culture might think: "Sure, it's great that we met our sales goal, but since I was responsible for more revenue than the other members of the team, I should receive a larger share of the annual bonus." In this mindset, if everyone gets an equal share of the bonus, people are tempted to coast along and not put maximum effort into their jobs. As a member of an individualistic culture, it is important that everyone receives the recognition due to him or her and, conversely, that everyone take responsibility for his or her mistakes.

A culture's inclination toward the group or the individual will be an important influence in areas such as teamwork, rewards and motivation, and decision-making.

Interacting with Americans

Americans pride themselves on their individualism. They like to be different, to stand out in a crowd. They are ingrained with the notion that each person should be responsible for his or her own actions. From infancy, American children are encouraged to make their own choices. When they grow up, many move far away from home. This mobility does not create an environment in which closely-knit extended families or groups of friends can survive. Instead, it fosters a strong sense of individuality.

Americans, along with Australians, are among the most individualistic cultures in the world. This is in direct contrast to group-oriented cultures, such as Japan. Other countries, such as Mexico, Greece, and France, are found in the mid-range of the continuum.

The United States and Group Cultures

People in group-oriented cultures have an individual identity, of course. However, the group plays an important role in making decisions, setting goals, and so on. And it is in these areas that miscommunications and conflicts can arise when someone from a group-oriented culture interacts with individualistic Americans.

Kazushi Yamaguchi, our protagonist in the scenario above, is not comfortable with the American practice of brainstorming. In Japan, it is risky—and potentially embarrassing—to present an idea to colleagues, and especially to superiors, in a public forum unless you already know their reactions. This means that when Kazushi has an idea, he will first feel out his peers and his supervisor. He will tweak his idea based on their private feedback and will present the idea in a meeting only when he has received everyone's support.

This type of consensus decision-making has the benefit of allowing for fast action; after all, everyone has already been informed and has agreed to the proposal. However, this approach is not compatible with many aspects of the American culture.

The same holds true for other circumstances where group and individual orientation come into conflict. Both team and individual competition is encouraged from childhood in both physical and mental prowess. Awards are usually given to individuals, not teams: to the sales person who had the highest sales or to the person who grew the largest tomato. Even team sports have an individual aspect; after all, even though the team wins the Super Bowl or the conference title, there is always a Most Valuable Player!

The United States and Individualistic Cultures

It is more difficult to differentiate between the United States and other countries that are also largely individualistic. Here, the difference is largely in the nature of individualism. In the United States, most people view individualism as the freedom—and indeed the right—to do whatever they please. This right stops just short of outright law-breaking.

In many other cultures, while they are largely individualistic, there are some elements of group orientation. Although people are responsible for their own actions, they also have some responsibility to society and to their neighbors. In fact, this responsibility may even be dictated by law. For example, a German who wants to crank up his stereo will have to bow to the wishes of his neighbors who have expressed the wish for a designated quiet time.

The importance of expressing one's individuality versus conforming to societal norms is taught at an early age. An American child who is coloring a picture can color the sky purple or green if she so desires. A German child might be told that since the sky is blue, she must color it blue. You might say, then, that Americans encourage individual expression while Germans allow themselves individual expression within the confines of societal norms.

Tips on American Individualism

- Individualism is both valued and expected in the United States. Success is measured on an individual level, not on a group level.
- Be prepared for competition in the workplace for everything from clients to promotions. This brings with it an element of self-advertisement, so don't be shy about declaring your accomplishments (but don't cross the line by showing off).
- Americans revel in their freedom of individual expression, but even more so in their right to do and say as they please.

STATUS & HIERARCHY

When he graduated from the university, Ferdinando Castelli entered an American company's management training program as an associate. Shortly after he arrived, his boss asked him to get some marketing statistics from a different department. Ferdinando had met Kyle Matthews, an American colleague who was also going through the program, during his orientation. Kyle was assigned to the other department, so Ferdinando called him to enlist his help in getting the information he needed. Kyle wasn't there, so Ferdinando left him a voice mail message. Later that day, when Ferdinando came back from lunch to find an voice mail message from Kyle, who said that he did not have the data Ferdinando needed and that he should

call Kathy Greene, the vice president of Kyle's department, who could get him the data. Ferdinando was puzzled by Kyle's unwillingness to help him and was unsure how to proceed; he didn't feel comfortable approaching a vice president.

Ascribed versus Achieved Status

Social strata are inherent in all cultures. How we differ is in the way we gain and attribute status. Do we acquire status by virtue of who we are or by what we do?

Status can be based on the inherent characteristics of a person, over which we have no control, such as age, race, gender, or family background. Or it may be based on what a person has accomplished, including educational and professional qualifications, such as the school one attended or whether one is a sign painter or a doctor.

Certainly, when we evaluate other people, we use a

mixture of these criteria. However, a culture generally values one over the other. In an ascribed-status culture, for example, an employee must show competence in order to advance in his or her job; however, he or she must also have seniority. The wisdom and experience that come with age are valued. Similarly, a manager might be influenced in his or her hiring decisions by the applicant's family background or social connections—or lack thereof. Social strata are generally well defined, and one does not easily move between them.

It is much more common in achieved-status cultures to accord status based on accomplishments. Social strata are less defined, and it is not uncommon to move up the social ladder. While there are certain benefits that come with seniority, it is possible for younger employees to be promoted above their elders. A person's past and, perhaps more importantly, potential future performance is valued above age. Many U.S. companies, in fact, have a certain number of "fast track" employees who are expected to move up quickly through the ranks based on their potential performance.

Vertical versus Lateral Hierarchy

Another aspect of status is whether the hierarchical structure is vertical or lateral. Hierarchy is something that exists in all cultures, whether hidden or overt.

In a vertical hierarchy, the structure tends to be overt. Positions within the hierarchy, corporate or social, are clearly outlined, and it is expected that people show and receive the respect due to them as a result of their position within the hierarchy. This respect is shown in many ways, from the use of titles to the depth of one's bow to the vocabulary one uses. The expatriate manager who tries to get his subordinates to call him "Dave" in a vertical hierarchy probably isn't going to have much luck—his employees will feel uncomfortable using such a disrespectful, familiar form of address to their boss. The title "Mr. Dave" may be the closest his subordinates come to using his first name.

Lateral hierarchies allow more equality among colleagues. Each person must be respected for his or her ability, regardless of position in the company. The more egalitarian nature of lateral hierarchies usually means a more informal environment. Lateral hierarchies also allow for greater empowerment at lower levels, as most decisions related to their jobs are made by employees themselves with less direct instruction from superiors. There is less concern for following the exact lines of authority than there is for finding the person who is in a position to take care of the issue at hand. Therefore, an employee who needs information from someone in another part of the business would have the freedom to approach that person directly, rather than channeling the request up through his boss, then on to the other person's boss, and finally down to the person who has the information, a restriction that an employee in a hierarchical organization would find difficult to circumvent.

You will find that a culture's views of the nature and importance of status influences business in the relationship and interaction between superiors and subordinates, in the way that information flows (or does not flow) between individuals, in the decision-making process, and in how people move up through the ranks, to name but a few issues.

Interacting with Americans

The United States falls toward the achieved-status side of the pendulum, and Americans tend to have a more lateral hierarchy. Australia and New Zealand are two cultures that are less status-oriented and hierarchical than the United States. In contrast, countries that are quite hierarchical and status-oriented are India and Japan; many other countries fall in between these extremes.

Most Americans expect to be promoted quickly regardless of their age, and promotions are usually based solely on performance. While you will probably get a raise in your salary every year, you are not likely to get promoted simply for having seniority.

One indicator of a vertical hierarchy is the use of more formality and titles, something not especially common in American companies. Most people are called by their first name no matter what their position: most supervisors call their subordinates by their first names and vice versa. If you call a company for customer service, you may be called Mr./Ms. [Last Name], but you are equally as likely to be called by your first name.

American organizations tend to have fairly flat structures with few levels. Because of this, it is common to find people in their 30s holding the title of manager or vice president. In fact, many organizations have an overabundance of middle managers, which can render the title virtually meaningless. In general, Americans don't mind jumping people in the line of authority if it is necessary to get the job done.

Despite this seeming equality within the organizational structure, salaries between the levels can vary greatly. The difference in the wages of the lowest paid and the highest paid employee is often in the hundreds of thousands of dollars.

On the home front, the American social hierarchy is fairly flexible. The remnants of a social structure do exist; America does have its royalty in the form of families such as the Kennedys and the Carnegies. And, of course, there are wide gaps in income, with some people making millions while others live in poverty. However, while there is some privilege in belonging to a wealthy family or attending a prestigious school, most Americans also believe that it is possible to achieve whatever you want, no matter what your background, subscribing to the adage "Where there's a will, there's a way." Many of America's heroes come from humble beginnings and are revered as much for overcoming the odds as they are for their accomplishments. In fact, most people are more impressed with an ordinary person who worked hard to fulfill his or her dream; Bill Gates, the founder of Microsoft, and basketball player Michael Jordan are just two examples of people from ordinary families who made their own places in the world.

The United States and Hierarchical Cultures

Whether or not one is comfortable with it, one of the first things that most people notice about the United States is that almost everyone is addressed by their first name. For some people from hierarchical cultures, American egalitarianism brings with it a freedom of speech and action that is not possible in their home countries. For others, it is a sign of disrespect and of a general lack of structure. No matter how you feel about it, egalitarianism is an integral part of the American psyche. It is in black and white in the first sentence of the U.S. Constitution, "We hold these truths to be self evident, that all men are created equal . . . ." Whether or not true equality has been achieved in the United States is a matter of debate; still, it is a goal that most Americans strive toward.

Working within the American business structure can be challenging. People from hierarchical cultures often find it difficult to adapt to an environment where the boss might be younger than his or her subordinates. For someone who values seniority and experience as much as ability, it can be difficult to see a relative newcomer to the company promoted or even to see someone hired into a senior position from the outside. Your American colleagues probably feel some of the same frustrations; you will hear grumbling when someone is promoted to a job they thought they should have been offered or if the company hires from outside of the company instead of promoting from within. This is one cause of what has become the norm in American business: frequent job changes.

However, working in a more egalitarian setting can also be quite liberating. Because the levels between the top and bottom of the company have been streamlined, and because it is not necessary to go through channels for routine tasks, many things can be accomplished quite efficiently. If you need information from someone, you can ask that person directly; if you make a request of someone, they are probably empowered to fulfill your request without getting approval from a higher-up.

The United States and Egalitarian Cultures

Although the U.S. business structure is flatter than most, there is a hierarchy, and it must be respected in many cases. Although you may be empowered to prioritize your tasks and to do your job as you see fit, your supervisor will probably want to be kept informed. It is common to copy your boss on e-mails and interoffice memos and to give him or her regular updates on your progress. It is important to note, however, that problems are often solved within the hierarchy rather than outside of it. For example, if you have a problem with your coworker, you can either approach your coworker directly or you can ask you manager to intervene. However, if you have a problem with someone in a different department or division, it is more common to ask your supervisor to address the issue with the supervisor of the other department.

Tips on Status and Hierarchy

- Most Americans are not overly concerned with social hierarchy. However, there are certain indicators of social status, including where one lives, where one went to school, and the number of luxury items (i.e., a boat, expensive car, etc.) one owns.
- Although the hierarchy in American companies tends to be fairly flat, it does play a role in business. It is important to go through the proper channels for some things, such as resolving a problem with a coworker or client. In the everyday operation of business, there is much contact between people at different levels; you can contact someone directly when their input is necessary for you to do your job.
- In theory, everyone should be treated equally. Realistically speaking, however, the higher your position is, the more weight your requests carry. In the business environment this translates to prioritizing the requests of the highest-ranking people.
- The role of supervisors and managers is generally more to provide direction and guidance than to instruct subordinates on the details of their tasks. Supervisors and subordinates generally communicate with each other as equals.
- If you are in a supervisory position, make sure you know the limits of your subordinates' job descriptions. For example, most

managers who have an assistant or secretary still read and respond to their own e-mail. Your assistant's job may not include
tasks like getting your coffee or picking up your dry cleaning.

RELATIONSHIPS

*Wong Yen Yen, who used the name Jenny Wong in the United States,
was on a business trip with her manager, Nancy Martin. Jenny was
slated to take over the Midwest sales region, and this was her first meeting with the company's most important clients. Jenny and Nancy were
traveling to Chicago and then to Minneapolis on a three-day trip.
Jenny asked Nancy if this was enough time, but Nancy assured her
that they would be fine. By the end of the whirlwind trip, Jenny was
feeling frustrated and a little anxious. After all, they had met with
three clients in each city; with all of the travel time necessary, they had
spent less than an hour with each client. Jenny felt like she needed more
time to get to know her clients, especially the big accounts. How could
her company expect her to establish a relationship in just one hour?*

What takes priority in your everyday business: your personal relationships or the tasks you perform? If you are from a relationship-oriented culture, relationships come before tasks, and, in fact, may be necessary in order to perform tasks. This can have many implications. A sickness in the family (even the extended family) may take precedence over work; a chance meeting with a friend might delay a scheduled meeting; a deal might not be struck until both parties have had time to build a basis of mutual respect and trust. Relationships—ones that go beyond just working together—are the cornerstones of a life of interdependent networks and are goals in and of themselves.

Task-oriented folks, on the other hand, tend to focus on the job at hand and leave the relationships to whatever time is left over after the work is finished. No friendship or personal intimacy is necessary to perform your job, and it is generally considered more professional not to let your personal life intrude on work. The general rule is that you should get on with your business and worry about "being friends" later.

This is not to say that relationship-builders don't get things done, nor is it meant to imply that task-focused people are not friendly. It simply means that the expectations you have of your personal and business relationships might not be the same as what is expected in another culture. If you are doing business abroad, you will find that these differences can be crucial to your success. You will see them crop up in negotiating, making deals, getting information, making sales, joint ventures, and team building, to name but a few areas.

Rule-Abiding versus Rule-Bending

A subset of the relationship-versus-task puzzle is the issue of relationships vis-à-vis rules. Should rules (this includes both actual laws and the unwritten rules of society) have a universal application, or is there room to maneuver or even circumvent them?

The United States is a country with a belief in the validity of rules, both written laws and unwritten rules. However, this is mitigated by the more important emphasis on individuality. Therefore, rules are not applied universally but are based on circumstances. For example, although it is against the law to cross the street outside of a crosswalk, people feel that if there are no cars coming or if traffic is at a stand-still, they can freely cross the road. Other rules are less easily broken; these are usually rules that involve other people. For instance, Americans instinctively stand in line for almost everything, even when there is no designated queue. So the rule that applies in the bank, where there are ropes to keep people in line, also applies to the bus stop, where there are none.

Unfortunately, the unwritten rules are often difficult to know, since they are instinctive and people often do not realize they are applying a rule. As a newcomer, you must be quite observant to learn all of the rules.

Rule bending has its limits, although these limits are often difficult to define. For example, most Americans don't feel guilty taking home pens or paper from their office, although they would never steal them from a store. It seems, then, that the line between rule abiding and rule bending is individually drawn and can be redrawn under a different set of circumstances.

Interacting with Americans

Americans are quite task oriented. Relationships play only the smallest of roles in their business lives. Like the United States, Germany, Austria, and the Netherlands are countries that fall on the task side of the continuum. In countries such as China, Japan, Saudi Arabia, and Brazil, relationships are very important.

In the United States, a small company looking for someone to design a Web site for them will spend time finding a company whose work and prices they like. Even though the Web designer will be responsible for a major part of the company's public image, there is no need for there to be any kind of bond between the two companies or their representatives. In fact, in today's environment, this transaction could be completed with no face to face contact. Initial contact can be made by phone or e-mail, the details and contract terms can be worked out in the same way, and the contract can be delivered via e-mail, signed, and mailed back. The cement that holds this business deal together is not a personal loyalty or trust, but a signed contract, probably valid for only a short period of time. If the company decides that it does not like the work of the Web designer or if it simply finds a better price elsewhere, it can move its business when the contract expires or pay a penalty for early termination.

Relationships do form in business, of course, but they are generally formed after a deal has been made, and they are often temporary. For example, if a sales representative forms a working relationship with his buyers, then moves to a new company, he does not expect his customers to move their accounts to his new company. He will probably contact them and win their business for his new company, but he will do so on the basis of better prices and service, not because of any personal loyalty. Therefore, business relationships can be fleeting, and they are usually only maintained as networking resources that may come in handy in the future, such as when one is looking for a new job.

Americans, of course, have friends, but most find it easy to blend their professional and personal lives. Coworkers will discuss their personal lives at work—their families, hobbies, and even romantic relationships. A typical topic of conversation at an American party is one's job. Americans often further the mingling of their work and personal lives by socializing with their coworkers outside of the business environment.

It is also important to address the way Americans build relationships, since this is an area that often perplexes newcomers. Think of American friendships as a peach. There is a soft skin that is easily broken; underneath there is meat of the fruit, juicy and sweet. But in the center of the peach you find the impenetrable pit. Americans are friendly people, and it's usually easy to meet people in the United States. Americans are quick to refer to people as friends, even when "acquaintance" would be a better word to describe the relationship. Americans, however, are uncomfortable with the word acquaintance, so a person they have known for only a few hours becomes a "friend." Many newcomers find that while it is easy enough to reach friendly terms with American friends, there is always a part of them that is unreachable, a core that is shielded. Perhaps this is because America is a very mobile society, where people move several times in their life, often from one part of the country to another. This makes it more difficult to establish and sustain the deepest bonds of friendships.

The United States and Relationship Cultures

The conflict between American task orientation and relationship-oriented cultures often causes misperceptions in how each views the other. To people from relationship-oriented cultures, the American business environment can seem cold and impersonal. There is more emphasis on contractual obligations than there is on establishing a mutual trust. In fact, the business itself seems to take on an identity in the United States. Employees revolve through various positions and several companies, but the company remains constant.

Because Americans do not feel the need to get to know someone personally before doing business, they are often impatient with people who are seeking to build a relationship. They view this practice as a waste of time and seek to steer the conversation in the direction of business and to push deals through quickly.

Very often, people from relationship-building cultures are confused by the duality of the American environment. On the surface, they see that their American colleagues are friendly, and that they are willing to talk about personal things, such as their families. As much as they blend their personal and professional lives, however, in the United States, one is supposed to also be able to separate business from personal feelings. A newcomer might therefore be bewildered when the supervisor with whom he thought he had established a relationship hires someone from the outside instead of promoting him. It is important not to confuse the characteristic friendliness of Americans as a relationship that carries any obligation.

The United States and Task Cultures

Even people who are comfortable in a task-oriented environment find it difficult to reconcile American friendliness with their need to get things done. The American business environment is overlaid with a veneer of friendship that seems to be at odds with their task orientation. For example, a newcomer to the United States might feel that the American propensity for discussing personal topics at work is inappropriate. However, a casual, friendly environment is typical of American offices, and someone who does not participate in a little friendly banter in the halls or gossiping at the coffee machine is usually viewed as cold and aloof—ironically the same way that Americans are characterized by their relationship-building colleagues.

Tips on Relationships

- The task comes first. Americans will quickly become impatient if you spend too much time on social conversation at a meeting or on the telephone. They will quickly bring the conversation around to business.
- If you would like to build a friendship with a coworker, suggest that you go out to lunch or for a drink after work. But be prepared for the conversation to revolve largely around work, especially at first.
- "It's just business" tends to be the business credo. This means that people are expected to separate their business decisions from their personal feelings.
- Be open to friendships but respect the boundaries your American friends might have. Remember that most people have many acquaintances that they might meet for coffee or for a night out only occasionally.
- Expect that your coworkers will talk about their families and other aspects of their personal lives. You can share as much or as little of your own life as you would like. But if you have a picture of your partner or family on your desk, your coworkers are sure to ask about them.

REASONING

Hans-Jürgen Straub was well-prepared for his presentation to the American subsidiary of his company. Hans-Jürgen was presenting the company's marketing strategy for its newest product, and his plan was to outline the steps that had led to the decision before moving on to the marketing aspects. He was only a few minutes into his presentation when he noticed that many of the audience members were fidgeting and glancing at their watches. Finally, Greg Martin, a senior-level manager at the American company, interrupted him, saying, "We're running a little short on time, Hans-Jürgen. Maybe you can just give us the bottom line and wrap things up."

Hans-Jürgen was astonished at the Americans' apparent lack of interest in his presentation, but he skipped most of the middle of his presentation and went directly to the strategy portion, which seemed to go over better. He thought that perhaps the Americans wanted to save time by reading the detailed documents he provided in lieu of the

presentation, but on his way out of the conference room, he noticed
that several people had tossed their material in the garbage can.

77

CULTURE

Pragmatic, Analytical, or Holistic Reasoning

Perhaps the most complex manifestation of culture is found in our thought processes. Around the world, the way people reason can be divided into three general styles: pragmatic, analytical, and holistic.

Pragmatic thinkers begin with the goal and seek the steps that will enable them to attain that goal. The emphasis is therefore on finding practical ways to solve a problem or reach a goal. For example, if the goal is to increase sales by 10% in a given year, the task is then to identify the means of doing so. A pragmatic thinker will, for example, compile information on increasing his or her client base and on the purchases made by current clients. The pragmatic thinker's final report might include a brief mention of all of the ideas that were presented, but its most prominent point will be the recommendation of certain sales strategies and how best to implement these strategies.

Analytical thinkers take the reverse approach, focusing on the process with the goal as the logical conclusion. An analytical thinker's approach to the problem of increasing sales by 10% will be different. He or she will begin by exploring all options, including increasing client base and increasing purchases. From there, the analytical thinker will select the strategies that will be the most beneficial, leading to the conclusion that it is possible to increase sales by 10% in a given year. This increase then becomes the goal.

Holistic thinkers incorporate both of the methods above, but they also tend to include elements in their thinking that most pragmatic and analytical thinkers would not. In determining sales, a holistic thinker would examine the information gathered on the potential and current client base, but he or she might also add a few things to the mix. For example, a holistic thinker may ask, what are the possibilities of expanding the current range of products? Even if the pragmatic and analytical thinkers above had thought of this scenario, it is much more likely to be in a linear fashion. That is, a seller of office products who is not a holistic thinker would not get into selling, say, women's lingerie. Holistic thinkers tend to be more non-linear in their thinking and may see a relationship between office products and women's lingerie that pragmatic and analytical thinkers do not, such as the fact that they have a ready supplier of both. Another example of a potential question asked by a holistic thinker is what the impact may be on the sales staff. Will the higher quotas require them to work more hours in the week or spend more time away from their families? Finally, after putting all of the pieces into the puzzle, the holistic thinker will see that it is possible to increase sales by 10%.

As you can see, each of the three scenarios above ended up in the same place: a 10% increase in sales. However, the road taken in each instance traveled through different terrain, even different countries. This difference in reasoning styles has an unmistakable impact on doing business abroad. Its significance is readily apparent in the process of decision-making, in writing reports and making presentations, and even in communicating.

Interacting with Americans

Americans are some of the world's most pragmatic thinkers. That is to say, Americans focus on "the bottom line," a phrase you'll hear often. Background information need not be extensively reviewed, since implementing a strategy to reach a goal is most important. The U.K. also falls within the category of pragmatism, while other European countries such as France and Germany tend to be classified as analytic thinkers. Asian countries such as Japan and India are good examples of countries where holistic reasoning styles are found.

The United States and Analytical Reasoning Cultures

American pragmatism often comes into conflict with analytical thought processes, where a review of background information is key to understanding the goals and is essential to developing a strategy. Americans are often frustrated by the amount of time necessary for detailed analysis, while their analytical counterparts often feel that Americans make decisions hastily and sometimes rashly.

Tell an American that the ice-cream store has decided to add a new flavor and he will start planning how to market it. Tell a German that the ice-cream store has decided to add a new flavor and he will want to know how the decision was reached—what research methods were used, what other flavors were tested, what the ingredients of the new flavor will be, etc. The American will eventually inquire about some of the details about the product research, and the German will begin working on the marketing plan once he has digested the background information. If they are working together, they will eventually arrive at a mutually agreeable marketing strategy and implementation plan, but not without some frustration on the part of both.

Generally speaking, Americans do not require a lot of detail, and would prefer to see the end result, while analytical thinkers prefer to have the whole picture. Analytical thinkers working with Americans often find them impatient and interested only in "the point," while the Americans find their analytical counterparts to be overly concerned with details.

The United States and Holistic Reasoning Cultures

American thinking tends to be linear, so the tangential thought process of holistic cultures is often difficult for Americans to comprehend. As a result, Americans might consider holistic colleagues to be unfocused or illogical. Conversely, holistic thinkers often find Americans to be too constrained in their thinking. Miscommunication, or even conflict, can arise when these two styles meet. In both cultures, it is important to consider the ripple effect of any decision. For an American, the pebble is dropped into a teacup, and the ripples go only to the edge of the cup. For a holistic thinker, the pebble is dropped into an ocean, and the ripples extend much farther and the impact can be felt in ways that the practical thinker cannot even imagine. For example, a Japanese person who wants to buy a car must take several things into consideration. In addition to finding a good car at a good price, he must also be careful to buy a car that corresponds to his status. That is to say, it is not a good idea to buy a more expensive car than the one driven by one's boss. An American, on the other hand, would not see any connection between the car he buys and his relationship with his boss; the choice of a car is totally individual and has no meaning within the context of the working relationship.

Tips on Reasoning

- Americans have a saying, taken from a 1960s television show: "Just the facts." There is more interest in the result than in how the result was achieved. Use summaries in place of detailed information and focus on the end goal.
- Practical thinking is valued. Rather than discuss why something happened, Americans prefer to find a way to fix it. By the same token, Americans tend to set goals quickly and modify them as necessary, rather than spend a great deal of time discussing the hows and whys of the goal.
- American decision-making is closely related to the other aspects of culture. They are convinced not by intangibles, such as the strength of your relationship or by your relative status, but by quantitative proof.

WHAT DOES IT ALL MEAN?

As you have probably already noticed, there are often correlations between the above categories. None of the six categories exists in a vacuum. If relationships are more important to you, it follows that you will be more willing to spend time (or waste it, from a task-oriented point of view) getting to know people before plunging into the task; relationship-oriented cultures tend to also be flexible-time cultures.

Similarly, if strong and harmonious relationships are your goal, that value will be reflected in the way you communicate; relationship-oriented cultures also tend to be indirect-communication cultures. You see the pattern.

In exploring the aspects of culture presented in this chapter, you may have realized that you have a lot in common with Americans—or that you have nothing in common with them! No matter where you see yourself on the cultural spectrum, you can be successful in the United States when you are armed with knowledge, practice, and, most of all, respect for the American culture. Chapters 6 and 7 will outline American business cultures and will give you some practical advice on living and doing business in the United States.

THREE

LIVING ABROAD

Most people face an international move with a combination of excitement and apprehension. Moving within the confines of your home country can be difficult enough; moving across borders adds a whole new dimension of cultural differences that can magnify the stress we all naturally feel in a new environment.

The single most important thing that you can do to ensure a successful sojourn abroad is to have realistic expectations. Unfortunately, it's difficult to gauge how realistic your expectations are before you go. You can, however, help define your perspective by considering the following points.

- **What do you hope to get out of your stay abroad?** If you will be working while you're abroad, your company will have certain expectations about the goals of your job, but it is up to you to set your own goals for personal and professional development. Be specific. Although "broadening my horizons" is an admirable goal, "gaining an understanding of the domestic automotive market" is a marketable skill that you will be able to use. If you will not be employed, it is essential that you make plans now for how you will occupy your time in the new country. What skills and interests do you have that you can apply to your advantage? You will have many options, including volunteering, continuing your education, or developing a hobby or skill into a freelance business.

- **If you have a partner and/or children, are you starting out with a sound relationship with your partner and with your children?** Although it may be tempting to regard an international assignment as a time to make a fresh start, it is not advisable to use the assignment to try to mend a troubled relationship. An inherent problem with living abroad is the stress caused by living in a new environment and the additional stress of confronting a foreign language and culture. A marriage or partnership that is in trouble, or a family with strained relationships, is more likely to crumble with the added pressure. Couples and families who start out with healthy relationships often find that their ties are strengthened by an international assignment. Each person is able to offer the support and encouragement necessary to create a positive environment with open lines of communication.

- **How much do you know about daily life in the country you are moving to?** It's one thing to know about the history of a country, to be familiar with the cultural icons, or to know where the best hotels are. But how much do you know about the infrastructure of the country? How much does it cost to live there? What is it like to go shopping? What is the definition of "service" in that country? Will you be able to find the foods you like, go to a nightclub alone or go skiing? In other words, will you be able to find all of the things that you count on to make your life easier and more pleasurable? And if you can't, can you live without them or find acceptable substitutes? These are very important questions to answer *before* you go. Most of the informa-

tion is not difficult to find if you are willing to look for it. You
can use the Internet, find books, or talk to people who have
lived there.

Of course, you may not be planning this relocation alone, and, if not,
there's a good deal to consider regarding your children and your
partner. We'll start with the children.

IMPACT ON CHILDREN

Accepting an international assignment is a decision that affects
everyone in your family, including children. Kids react in a variety of
ways, including excitement, resentment, and fear. Children can benefit enormously from living internationally. They develop the ability
to look at the world multi-dimensionally and interact successfully
with a wide variety of people; they also tend to be open-minded and
less judgmental. Unfortunately, at the beginning of an assignment,
those benefits are on a distant horizon. What you have to deal with
immediately is getting your children acclimated to their new lives as
painlessly as possible.

Any kind of move can be difficult for children; being uprooted
from friends and school and getting adjusted to a strange place is not
easy. With an international move, and the usual questions of Will anyone like me? and Will I be able to make friends?, children have to deal
with a new culture where kids may dress, speak, or act differently—or
all of the above. Fortunately, there are many steps you can take to
smooth the transition.

First of all, involve children in the decision to move abroad. That
is not to say that you must allow your child the chance to veto the
move. The first reaction of most children to any move—domestic or
international—is generally negative. (In fact, if a child reacts posi-
tively, it may be a sign of an underlying problem. Your child may be
viewing the move as an escape hatch.) But you can let your child
know as early as possible about the move. Take the time to discuss
why the move is necessary. This is especially important for older chil-

dren and teens. They are old enough to be involved in discussions about why this move will help Mom or Dad's career.

Secondly, let your child express all of his or her feelings about the move. A child's emotions will probably run the gamut from anger to excitement at one time or another. Share your own feelings, too. Let your child know that it's a little scary for you, too, but also exciting. Most importantly, let your child know that it's okay to feel anxious, excited, scared, or angry.

Another important way to help children adjust is to talk about expectations. Be optimistic, but prepare to accept the bad as well as the good. Don't hide the fact that it is going to be hard at times, but don't forget to emphasize the positive. Help your kids learn about their destination. Make it a family project in which you all participate. The more realistic your child's expectations are—and your own, too, incidentally—the less difficult the transition will be.

A good way to ease a transition abroad is to take items from the house and from your child's room that will make the new house or apartment feel like home. Continuity is a key factor in a child's adjustment. Even though it may be tempting to leave a lot of items and replace them when you get to your destination, try to take as many of your child's belongings as possible. It is worth the trouble of packing and shipping if your child's bicycle or his or her own familiar bed helps him or her to become comfortable with her new home.

Just as you involved your children in the decision to move, involve children in the actual move as much as possible. Children feel helpless during an international move. They are being moved abroad without having much say in the matter. It will help lessen the feelings of helplessness if you let children make as many decisions as you can. Let your child choose favorite toys or furniture, a favorite picture from the living room, or other items that you will take with you.

Allow your children the opportunity to say goodbye to their friends. Have a party and let the children invite their friends, or enlist the help of a teacher in throwing a class party. Take videos or lots of pictures to make an album to bring with you. Adults are sometimes surprised that young children have as deep an attachment to their playmates and possessions as older children. With all children, it is important to recognize the sense of loss and grieving that they go through when moving. Making "good good-byes" is an important step in being ready to accept the new.

Finally, make plans for staying in touch with family and friends. Make an address book for younger children to write down the addresses of their friends so that they can write. Think about other ways to stay in touch, such as a newsletter, faxing, e-mailing, or creating an audio- or videotape that you can send home. Create a schedule for a weekly or monthly telephone call, writing letters, or making your tapes.

There is no formula that you can use to determine how your child is going to react. And obviously, two children in the same family can have totally opposite reactions, with one skipping cheerfully off to school right away and one suffering stomach-aches that double him or her over in pain. Personality plays a part in the adjustment, but so do the parents and the environment created in the new home. Following are some descriptions of general behavior patterns. As you read these descriptions, consider how your child has reacted to stressful situations in the past—this will give you insight into how he or she might react to an international move, which is most assuredly stressful—and give some thought to how you can help him or her manage the cultural transition.

Infants and Toddlers

While the biggest disruption for infants is the change in sleeping and eating schedules, toddlers will have a harder time understanding what is happening and will require a great deal of reassurance, before, during, and after the move. Distress at this age often results in a regression to babyish, clinging behavior.

Preschoolers

Preschool-aged children should be involved in the move as much as possible. Create ways in which they can help, such as selecting which toys and clothing to bring and which to leave, labeling the boxes from his or her room, and packing for the trip. Seeing things being put into boxes and knowing that they will be unpacked in a few weeks is reassuring. Games will help explain the move; you can stage a play move with a dollhouse or by packing up and "moving" in your child's wagon. Coloring and activity books and picture books of your destination will add to the sense of security. Don't forget that shipped boxes may take several weeks to arrive. Make sure you take some familiar items on the plane for your child.

Preteens

Older children will have more questions and will require more explanations. Take the time to discuss why you are moving, and be open about your feelings about moving. It helps children to know that their parents are sad to be leaving behind the people they know but are looking forward to a new experience. Learn with your children about your new country. Make trips to the library and select books that you can read together. Get a world map and a map of the country so they can see where they are going. Work with your children's teachers to make a presentation about the country. Learn about the food, traditional clothing, or holidays of the country. You can also help your children learn some phrases in the new language. Make a game of learning how to say "please" and "thank you" and other simple phrases. And give older children as much responsibility as possible in getting ready to move.

Teens

Teenagers often have the most difficulty with a major move. They are at a time in their lives when they are trying to establish an identity separate from their families and gain independence. The identity being shaped is linked to friends and social activities; changes make things all the more difficult. Moving to another country adds more pressure in the form of a potential language barrier and unknown customs. The best way to help teenagers through this period is through open communication. Let them know that what they are feeling is okay. You can also help by finding out as much information as possible about where you are going. Get information on the new school, including the curriculum and extracurricular activities. Finding out how kids dress and what they like to do when they get together is important, too.

Although living abroad is a rewarding experience, some circumstances make it preferable to allow a teenager to remain behind for the remainder of a semester or a school year (especially for students in their last year of school). Include your teenager in the discussion and make the decision based on the needs of your family.

All children, no matter what age, pick up on and, to a certain extent, reflect the behavior of their parents. Therefore, a positive attitude on your part is the best way to influence your children. Your enthusiasm and acceptance of your new life will help them adjust. The way you handle your own frustrations will set the example for them.

IMPACT ON SPOUSES OR PARTNERS

In the majority of cases, expatriates who accompany their spouse or partner abroad are not able to get the necessary permit to work in the host country. If you are giving up or postponing a career or job to make this move with your partner, you are suddenly faced with a great deal of free time that you will have to occupy in the new country.

Giving Up or Postponing a Career

At first glance, having several months—or even several years—of free time may sound like a dream come true. In fact, there are probably few people who wouldn't welcome an extended vacation. However, you will find that after a couple of weeks of inactivity, you will begin to feel restless. For most people, a career provides a lot of their self-identity and a feeling of self-worth, and its absence will certainly leave a void.

Being a Stay-at-Home Parent

When there are children in the family, the accompanying partner often decides to give up his or her career with the expectation that staying at home with the kids will provide more than enough to do. Before making this decision, here are a couple of issues to consider.

- How old are your children?
- Will your children be attending school?
- If your children will be in school, how do you plan to occupy your time when they are gone?
- Are there ways to get involved with your children's activities (i.e., volunteering at the school, coaching, leading field trips, etc.)?

DUELING CAREERS

The most pressing concern for dual-career couples is usually finding a position for the accompanying partner. It is important to stress that, while it is not always possible to find a paid position, there are usually plenty of other opportunities. The best way to find a job while you are living abroad is to redefine what work is. Broaden your definition from a nine-to-five job to include a host of other things, such as volunteering (which may lead to a paid position), freelancing, consulting, continuing your education, or learning new skills.

The following questions will help you begin to plan for identifying an occupation while you are abroad.

- Is it possible to get the permit you need to be eligible to work in that country? Can your company or your partner's company help you obtain one?
- Are there any opportunities within your company in the new location (in a local office, if there is one; as a consultant; or working on a project for your company that can be accomplished from abroad)?

- Are there any similar opportunities within your partner's company?
- Are there entrepreneurial possibilities that you can pursue while abroad?
- Does either your company or your partner's company offer any type of career counseling or job location assistance that would help you find a suitable position abroad? (This can sometimes be negotiated as part of the relocation package.)
- Are there volunteer opportunities in your field that you would consider appropriate substitutes for a paid position?
- Are there other opportunities outside of your field that you would consider appropriate substitutes for a paid position?
- Do you have a hobby or another interest that you could capitalize on? For example, if you have an interest in photography, can you freelance or assist a professional photographer?
- Is this an opportunity to make a career change? You will have a period of time that you can put to use learning new skills or developing your skills in a different direction.

So far in this section, we've taken a look at some important points to remember when considering the impact of a move abroad on yourself, your children, and your partner. Another major issue is cultural adaptation, or, in other words, what you should expect as you look ahead at your and your family's acclimation to a new culture.

UNDERSTANDING CULTURAL ADAPTATION

Culture shock, or cultural disorientation, is the result of finding yourself in a culture that is new and unfamiliar. People in the new culture not only speak a different language, they also live by a different set of rules, with different values, attitudes, and behaviors. In some cases, these differences are immediately obvious; in others they are quite subtle. Cultural disorientation results in a range of emotional reactions, from irritation and frustration to anxiety and insecurity to resentment and anger. If the cultural adaptation process is not well managed, it will lead to depression.

No one is immune to culture shock; even frequent travelers and people who have lived abroad before feel its effect. The exception to the rule is the person who experiences mild culture shock in an abbreviated form. For the vast majority of sojourners, culture shock has a significant impact. The key to managing the cultural adaptation process is understanding what it is and developing an awareness of how it is affecting you personally. Once you reach this understanding, you will be ready to take steps to manage the stress caused by culture shock.

Culture shock is an emotional cycle with four distinct periods: enchantment, disenchantment, retreat, and adjustment. Although most people experience all four periods, each person's cycle is different; even different members of the same family will go through the ups and downs at different times.

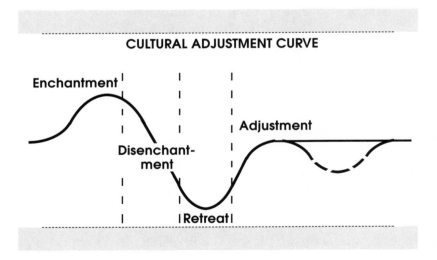

CULTURAL ADJUSTMENT CURVE

Enchantment

Adjustment

Disenchant-
ment

Retreat

Enchantment

Your arrival in your new home is an exciting time. Your senses are operating at top speed as you try to assimilate all of the new sights, sounds and smells. You want to see and do everything. There are many new things to learn and discoveries to make. The differences that you notice between your home country and your new country are charming.

Disenchantment

After several weeks, a period of disenchantment typically sets in. As you establish your routine in your new country, reality begins to intrude on your enchantment. You have to deal with the mail carrier, the plumber, and your neighbors. Even simple tasks become difficult. When you go shopping, you may not recognize the food, and you may not be able to find what you want and what you're used to. People may seem rude, overly friendly, or just plain different. It is emotionally taxing to speak a new language, to use a new currency, and to perform all of the other minor details that you never gave a second thought to at home. With the new reality comes a sense of frustration and irritation, and often insecurity, since all of the cues you never had to think about before have changed.

Retreat

As you begin to feel more and more frustrated, tension and resentment will begin to build up. The retreat stage of the adjustment cycle is the most difficult. It becomes harder to leave your home. If you work, you may find yourself working late or coming straight home from the office. You turn down invitations and minimize contact with the culture and people in the new country. What was once "charming" or "interesting" about the country and customs has become "strange" and "stupid." In the constant comparison between your home country and the host country, home always wins. Homesickness is acute.

Adjustment

Finally, you will have to make the effort to adjust, to reestablish contact with the world and go on with your life. Your attitude will determine how you reconcile yourself to the things that are different in your new country. The people who make the most successful adjustments are those who realize that there are things that you like and dislike in any culture; doubtless there are things that you didn't care for at home, too. If you are willing to accept the culture, enjoy the things that you love about the culture, and find ways to accommodate the parts that you do not like, you will be happy. Once you have managed a successful adaptation, you will realize that you have gained a new set of skills, and are able to operate effectively within a new culture.

And Beyond

If you take another look at the Cultural Adjustment Curve, you will notice a second dip. Many people experience a second low period, or even a series of ups and downs. Just when you think you've finally got things figured out, you stumble again. Subsequent periods of disillusionment might be more or less severe than the first; this reaction is normal.

KEYS TO A SUCCESSFUL ADJUSTMENT

The keys to a successful adjustment are self-awareness and acceptance. In order to be able to recognize cultural differences and effectively deal with them, you must first be aware of your own cultural values and attitudes.

Acceptance, the second key, means understanding that the culture, customs, and rules in your new country, however far from your home country, are valid. Once you are able to accept them as different, rather than better or worse than your own, you will be more comfortable and able to adapt to new ways of doing things.

Understand that the ups and downs of cultural adjustment are normal; everyone who has moved before you has experienced the same process, complete with similar symptoms. If you reach out to those people, they can help you through the process. They will tell you that they survived and so will you.

Even after you have adjusted, you will have good days, when you feel at ease in your new culture, and bad days, when you question your decision to move there. Once you have completely adjusted, the good days will eclipse the bad.

Coping Techniques

The psychological disorientation of an international move causes a tremendous amount of stress. In order to manage your cultural adaptation successfully, you must find an outlet for this stress. Think for a moment about how you relieve stress in your life right now. Stress outlets can be physical, such as jogging or biking, or mental, such as meditation or reading. List your stress relievers on a piece of paper. Once you've made your list, think about how you can continue those activities in your new home. Some of them—meditation, for instance—are easily transported. Some, however, may require modification or planning. For example, if you're used to riding your bike through the country lanes near your home but you will be moving to a crowded urban center, you may have to modify your activity. Can you use a stationary bike instead? Are there nearby parks or other areas where you can safely bike?

If you are not sure about the availability of a specific activity, make it a priority to find out. There are many resources, including other expatriates, people from your new country who may live in your area, consulates, books, and more.

FAMILIES

Families who have relocated to another country move with their own built-in support network to help each member through the process of adaptation. However, relocation also often means that family roles shift. A spouse who was a breadwinner before moving abroad might become a dependent; normally independent children may find themselves dependent on their parents, at least initially.

An international assignment often includes regional responsibilities that require frequent travel or extended business trips. If one partner is required to travel often, the other is left taking on more of the shared responsibilities in order to fill the gap left by the numerous absences. At times, one feels like a single parent, even if it's not the case! Of course, the partner who is frequently away can find himself or herself feeling left out of the family upon his or her return.

All of these changes can be successfully managed if you have open lines of communication. Parents will benefit by talking with each other about the changes that are necessary to accommodate the new situation and by discussing ways that they can support each other to maintain consistency. The whole family will function better if everyone feels comfortable expressing fears and concerns and receives encouragement and support from other family members.

THE NON-WORKING PARTNER

Unlike children and the working partner, a non-working partner faces a new life that is without the inherent structure of school or work. So once the initial settling-in is done, your partner goes to work every day, and the children head off to school, you are left with nothing to do. If you were used to working, this is especially difficult. Even if you were not employed prior to the move, you still have left behind all of the familiar routines that filled your day.

According to numerous articles, many unsuccessful assignments are attributed to a non-working partner who is unhappy in the new culture. This puts a lot of pressure on you; but with some effort and planning, you can put that particular worry aside.

In the absence of outside activities, the world of a non-working partner is limited to household chores and the lives of children and the spouse. In the initial months, these same children and spouses have spent the majority of the day coping with their own stresses in the new culture and are rarely in the mood for scintillating conversation when they return to the sanctuary of home.

The more activities that you are involved in, the more fulfilled your own life will be. These activities can include your family, such as volunteering at your child's school, or they can be a pursuit of your own interests. The possibilities are practically endless. Other than volunteering, you can use the spare time to take classes, develop new skills, or pursue a hobby. If you give your imagination free rein, there are plenty of things that you can do. See the dual career sections throughout the book for other ideas on making the most of your time abroad.

CHILDREN

Children go through their own adjustment process, just as adults do. Younger children often feel frightened in a new location where everything is different from what they are used to: the people may look different, buildings may look different, and things certainly sound and smell different. Sometimes children (and adults, too) become an object of curiosity if they are living in a country where they look very different from the locals (for example, a Japanese child in a small southern U.S. town). They are often uncomfortable being stared at closely scrutinized by curious strangers.

Younger children will have difficulty understanding what the move means and may tend to relate the move to vacations that they have experienced. They may be waiting for the trip to be over and for the family to return to their familiar surroundings at home. When the return home does not happen, they can get very upset. This may not happen for several weeks, or even months, so that a child who seems to have adjusted well might have problems down the road. Symptoms of their distress may be quite physical, such as stomachaches, or emotional, such as withdrawal and depression.

Older children, who do understand the implication of an international move and who realize that this move is not permanent, may be reluctant to get too deeply involved with friends, trying to protect themselves from the pain of making friends only to leave again after a year or two.

Throughout the process of adjustment, children will experience periods of anger. This is understandable since they have been dragged across the world against their wishes. It is important to allow children, whatever their age, to express their anger and to provide appropriate outlets for it.

Keep in mind, too, that younger children may not be able to put their feelings into words. You can help them express their feelings by taking along children's books about moving that will help them find the words to tell you what is wrong.

Naturally, all children will react differently to an international move. The best way to cope is with patience and understanding.

Global Nomads and Third-Culture Kids

Global nomads, also called third-culture kids, are those who have lived overseas before adulthood, usually because of a parent's job. The global nomad is abroad without choice; the parents have chosen an international lifestyle, usually with the expectation that they will eventually return to the passport country. When children live abroad for a long period of time—or even for fairly short periods of time— they become culturally different from the parents. Their whole avenue of cultural exploration is very different from that of one born and reared in one place (as the parents often are).

Living internationally is a unique opportunity for children. It is a heritage that will shape the rest of their lives. While overseas, children develop a whole host of global skills, including multilingual skills, the ability to view situations from two different sides, mediating skills, and cross-cultural skills—simply by living. It is a heritage that can be applied very usefully in today's global arena.

One of the biggest challenges of moving abroad is maintaining the cultural identity of children. Children are absorbing the new culture through school, from care givers, and from what they observe in the world around them. "Home" becomes a place to go on vacation once or twice a year. Parents can keep children connected to their own culture in a variety of ways, such as observing the holidays and traditions of their home culture. It is also helpful to keep in contact with what's going on at home, both with friends and family members and through magazines and newspapers.

PARENTING ABROAD

Raising a child abroad is a special challenge. Depending on where you are living, the values may be different than those you want to instill in your children. Children learn not only from their parents, but from school, peers, other caregivers, and society in general. Imagine that you have told your teenagers that they must be a certain age before they can drink, but they are suddenly confronted with vending machines in Japan that sell whiskey with no restrictions. This doesn't mean that Japan has a rampant problem with teenage alcoholism; it simply indicates that Japanese children are governed by different societal and parental restraints than your child. These kinds of problems are best dealt with by establishing very clear family rules. Have family meetings to establish and reinforce the rules.

A lack of organized activities for teenagers is often a problem. You and your child may have to actively search for the activities he or she likes to do. If you can't find appropriate activities, think about organizing a baseball team, a drama group, or other activities yourself. Encourage your children to bring their friends over, and try to meet their friends' parents, just as you would at home.

In some countries, the expatriate life itself can pose hazards in the form of making children accustomed to a higher standard of living than most people. Some people find themselves in a position to obtain household help. If you have never had this experience, it will take some time to be comfortable having someone work for you. You may have to train the people you hire, and you should definitely be clear on your expectations; do not assume, for example, that your idea of disciplining your children is shared by the person you hire to babysit your child.

If you are lucky enough to have household help, you may find that your children come to expect that someone will pick up after them and believe that they are not personally responsible for any chores. If that is contrary to what you want your children to learn, you may want to continue to assign some household tasks to children to reinforce your own values to them.

DUAL-CAREER COUPLES

Dual-career couples with children face the same issues as other families, but with an additional concern: child care. You are leaving behind your own child-care network and will have to rebuild it from scratch. This can be complicated, especially if your extended family plays a major role in child care or if you are in a country where public or private child care is rare. Even if your children are in school, there may not be structured activities for them to participate in during the time between school and the end of the work day. There are options if you search for them. Think about the following ideas:

- Hire an au pair, nanny, or other live-in help.
- Look for formal or informal networks within the expatriate community; often there is a system of sharing child care.
- If your job has the flexibility, work from home or part time.
- Approach a neighbor or another family about looking after your child during the day.
- Find an older person who would be interested in caring for your child (this has the added benefit of providing your child with a "grandparent").

If you are not able to find viable child care options, you may be able to create something that will meet your needs. And there are sure to be other families who would welcome the alternative. Don't rule out starting a day-care center for younger children or organizing after-school activities for older children.

The most important thing, of course, is that you feel comfortable with your child-care arrangements and that you trust the person who will be caring for your children.

THE SINGLE LIFE

Living abroad as a single person has both ups and downs. Moving to a place where you have no network of friends is difficult; coping with a new country and culture where you may not know how to go about meeting people to create your new social network is even tougher. In many countries, a person's work and home lives are kept quite separate. Social bonds have been formed throughout the years in school and elsewhere; business relationships do not necessarily translate into social relationships. And, in many cases, the family and extended family play a significant role in a person's life, and a great deal of time is spent in family activities. All of this can make it seem impossible for a newly arrived person to meet people and form friendships.

On the other hand, expatriates are often not subject to the same rules as everyone else. Most expatriates find people in their host country to be very sympathetic to their situation, interested in learning more about them, and open to the possibilities of a relationship that extends beyond office hours. With luck, you will find yourself the recipient of invitations from your colleagues.

In the final analysis, though, it is up to you to build your new life. There are many avenues open to you. The best way to meet people, in fact, is to simply do something that you like to do. If you like to hike, go hiking; if you like to work out, join a gym. By doing something that interests you, you are putting yourself in situations where you can meet people with the same interests.

Another possibility to explore is the expatriate community. Where there are significant numbers of expatriates, there are usually networks in place, both for business and social purposes. Often there is a newcomer's club that provides activities and events for socializing. In these organizations, too, you will find people who have gone through the relocation and adaptation process and who have first-hand knowledge of what you are experiencing. These can be invaluable contacts throughout your own process of adaptation, giving you the support and encouragement you need, or even a shoulder to cry on when necessary.

Singles often have a unique experience abroad. Because they are not accompanied by a family, they generally have much more contact with the language and culture of the host country. An expatriate with a family goes home at the end of the day, speaks his or her native tongue at home, and is shielded from the language and culture to some extent. A single person does not have that shield and spends more time speaking the new language and immersing himself or herself in the culture through his or her social life. That person often has the added benefit of learning the language more quickly and thoroughly and of adapting to the new culture quickly.

SEXUAL ORIENTATION

If you are lesbian or gay, you will probably want to do some research on the acceptance of homosexuals in the country you will be living in before you embark on your international assignment. While some countries have laws preventing discrimination against anyone because of sexual orientation, the acceptance of homosexuals by the society in general ranges from tolerance to homophobia. Make sure you are also aware of any laws prohibiting homosexual acts, and the possible consequences of practicing your sexuality. These concerns will affect bisexuals and transgendered people as well.

In the United States, homosexuality is openly discussed and widely accepted in certain areas. However, this does not mean that you will not experience discrimination if you are open with your sexuality, especially in small town. Moving abroad with a same-sex partner presents certain challenges not faced by married partners, as it is virtually impossible for an accompanying partner to get a work visa without being legally married. In addition, few companies include same-sex partners in the expatriate benefit package, causing complications in matters such as housing allowances, insurance, and allowances for the loss of the partner's income.

As an accompanying partner, you must focus on the alternatives that are available to you in the new country. Issues of giving up or postponing a career must be dealt with, and work alternatives must be investigated. Be proactive in exploring your options. Try to talk to people who have experience living in the country, both natives of the country and expatriates who have lived there. The more people you can talk to, the more complete a picture you will have about the implications of being lesbian, gay, bisexual, or transgendered in your new culture.

RACE AND GENDER QUESTIONS

Many people find that when they move abroad, they are confronted by different ideas and attitudes about race and gender. Some find that they have suddenly become part of a racial minority in their new country, or they encounter challenges that did not exist at home as a result of racial differences. Women and men alike may find themselves in a culture where gender roles are very different from what they are used to; both may need to adjust to different ideas of gender equality. Because these questions vary significantly from country to country, they are important topics to address no matter where you are moving. You can find more information on these topics in the "Living and Staying in the United States" and "Business Environment" sections of this book.

A WORD ABOUT "EXPATRIATE CLUBS"

Many expatriates are wary of expatriate clubs, seeing them as a group of spouses who get together to play tennis and bridge. Even if there are people in the organization who do play bridge, the clubs are much more than that. Expatriate organizations are an excellent source of information on everyday issues, such as finding a doctor, networking for accompanying partners who are seeking jobs or alternatives, cultural learning through structured activities and events, and socializing. Each individual can decide how much he or she wants to be involved in the expatriate community. Indeed, there are plenty of expatriates who immerse themselves in it and have very little contact with local-country nationals. There are also people who avoid it altogether. You are free to choose either, or any point in between. Just keep in mind that the expatriate network can be invaluable; it can also provide that touch of home when you need it.

STAYING IN TOUCH

Even if you are excited about the prospect of living abroad, don't forget to make plans to stay in touch. You will want to hear from your family and friends at home, and keep them up-to-date on your own adventures. It's very easy to get swept up in your new life, and difficult to find the time to write or call with all of the new challenges of living abroad. However, the people who form your network of support will continue to be important as you adjust to your life abroad, especially during difficult times.

Establishing and maintaining a systematic way of communicating with home is also critical when it comes time to return after your sojourn abroad—something that is difficult to think about when you haven't even left yet!

It would be a good idea to pass on your new address to your friends and relatives a month before you leave for the United States. Depending on where it originates, international mail can take two weeks or more to get through; the better option comes through the immediacy of e-mail correspondence. Regular correspondence, especially in the first month after your arrival, provides an outlet for emotions and may well prevent you from feeling isolated.

ROUND-TRIP TICKET: THE RETURN HOME

Contrary to what you might think, the return home, or repatriation, after an international assignment is often a more difficult transition than moving abroad.

Professional Repatriation

One of the hazards of living and working internationally is that when you return, you can find yourself out of touch with your home office and with changes in your field or profession. Without proper preparation, you may find yourself without an office, without direction, and, indeed, without a job. Many former expatriates have returned home after a successful assignment only to have to wait for a suitable position to open up. In addition, many returned expatriates find that their experience abroad and their newly acquired skills and knowledge are not put to use by the organization. A marketing manager fresh from an assignment in the United States may find himself or herself in a domestic marketing position with little or no involvement in any global markets. Even if the goal of the assignment was your professional development with an eye toward "globalization" or developing the international market, it is difficult to put those lofty goals to work practically. It is up to you to ensure that you are receiving the support you need during the assignment and to plan your strategy for reintegration into the home or local office.

If you moved abroad with your partner but were unable to work abroad, you face some of the same challenges when you return. You may feel that technology has passed you by or that the skills you used before you moved are rusty from disuse. The best way to counteract this is to think about coming home while you are abroad and make sure that you keep your skills up-to-date—and maybe even develop new skills or expertise!

Following these steps can ease your professional reentry:

- Set a strategy before you go. Getting the support of upper management is crucial. Make sure you have a clear understanding of the objective of sending you abroad, what your goals are during the assignment, and exactly how you will fit back into the organization when you return.

- Stay in touch while you are abroad. In the case of international assignees, "out of sight, out of mind" holds true more often than not. Remind the home office of all of the points outlined above. Keep them informed about what you are doing and your accomplishments. And keep yourself informed about what is going on at the home office, promotions and staff changes, important policy changes, etc. E-mail and faxes are readily available in most companies; take advantage of technology to maintain contact.

- Find a mentor. In fact, find two or three. Mentors will help keep you in the minds of the decision and policy makers and keep you informed about what's going on at home. Mentoring relationships do not have to be formalized. And by finding several mentors, you won't find yourself returning from your assignment only to find that your champion in the company no longer works there!

- Visit the home office whenever you can. While you are on a home leave or business trip back, take the opportunity to reconnect with colleagues. Make use of the time to familiarize yourself with recent changes.

Even if you take all of the recommended steps to stay in touch, understand that things will be different when you return. The fact is, the company and your colleagues have grown in the time you have been away, just as you have. It will take time and patience to reintegrate yourself into the new environment.

Personal Repatriation

Personal repatriation can also be painful. During your sojourn, you will have gained new insights and new perspectives. You will realize that there is really no right or wrong way to do things, only different ways. In addition, most people remember home with fondness while they are away, forgetting about the things that aren't so great. And, of course, you will come home to find that your home country has its share of blemishes, just like everywhere else. This means that you will go through another cycle of adjustment as you refamiliarize yourself with your home culture and come to terms with the bad as well as the good in it.

If you are gone for several years, you will experience some disorientation when you return. Things will have changed, and you will have had a long period of time that you have not shared experiences with your family and friends. You may find that some people aren't interested in hearing about your experiences abroad, or who roll their eyes when you say, "When I was in . . . ." You may even encounter people who feel that you are putting on airs or that you feel superior because of your experience. You will have to come to terms with the fact that the people you knew before you left have changed, as you have, but in different ways.

There are ways to ease your personal readjustment.

- Stay in touch while you are gone. This can be difficult as you immerse yourself in your new life. Just as you fade from prominence at home, home fades for you. You will have to make a conscious effort to maintain regular contact, and make sure your kids do. The benefit of doing this is that when you return, there is less of a void in your experiences; you have kept people informed of important events in your lives, and vice versa.
- Visit home whenever possible. This is especially important if you have children. In addition to helping you keep in contact with friends and family, it helps children maintain their sense of "home" and their cultural identity.
- Realize that your return home will have its ups and downs, just as your adjustment to living abroad did.

Children's Repatriation

The most difficult part of readjustment for children is that they have a gap in their lives where they have missed all of the pieces of popular culture that their friends have experienced, such as music, movies, TV, toys, and the way kids dress. They have to learn the current slang and how kids talk. Along with this, they are different from their peers. They have developed in ways that kids at home have not, and they have a different frame of reference. More than adults, children who return home after living abroad will find that their peers see them as thinking that they are superior and resent references to, "When I was in . . . ."

Tips for Staying in Touch

Most of us are accustomed to picking up the telephone and calling someone whenever we want. If you are living in another country, though, you may find that this isn't as easy any more because of time differences, poor international phone service, or the prohibitive cost of international calls. Here are some suggestions for alternative ways of staying in touch.

- **The old stand-by: write letters.** Since the advent of the telephone, most of us are no longer letter-writers. When phoning is too expensive, this is one of the cheapest alternatives. However, it's also the slowest!

- **Chatting online.** If you and your family/friends all have Internet access and you are able to access the Internet from your new country, try scheduling a time to chat online in chat rooms or through an instant message program. Some of the larger services, such as MSN and AOL, offer instant message software. Just remember that you may have to pay for local connect time rates; check with your Internet service provider.

- **E-mail.** Probably the least expensive alternative, although not an option for everyone.

- **Fax letters.** Write your letter, then fax it. This will give you the satisfaction of instantaneous communication without the prohibitive cost of an extended telephone call. Family and friends without a fax machine may be able to arrange to receive faxes at work or elsewhere.

- **Use the company's phone.** With the company's permission, of course! As part of the expatriate package, some companies will allow you and your family members limited use of office phones to make international calls.

- **Videotapes or cassettes.** Although it will take a while to get there, videotapes and cassettes are more personal than writing letters. It's especially nice if you have children. You can exchange tapes with family members, and your children can exchange them with friends and even their classmates at school. Be sure you will have access to the right equipment, since many countries use PAL instead of VHS. A further word of caution: be careful not to run afoul of the local laws. For example, in some countries, a videotape that includes your sister frolicking on the beach in a bikini may be considered pornography locally, even if you don't think it is. Make sure you know all of the applicable laws.

- **Write a newsletter.** This is especially helpful if you've got a long list of people you want to keep in contact with. Document what is happening in your life, write about the funny things that happen, about current events in your new community, or anything else that appeals. Or start a round-robin letter, where everyone who receives the letter adds to it and passes it on to the next person.

- **Create a family Web site.** If you have a little bit of Internet know-how and some time on your hands, this can be a fun and creative way to display pictures, news, even sound clips for family in other parts of the world to enjoy.

- **Schedule regular phone calls.** It's bad enough to reach an answering machine when you want to talk to someone. It's worse when you are paying international rates to talk to a machine! If you talk to someone often, try to arrange for a regular time to call—every Sunday night at 10:00, the last Saturday of each month, or whatever fits both of your schedules.

LEARNING ABOUT YOUR NEW HOME

You're on your way to a new adventure. Now is the time to gather all of the information you need to make your international sojourn successful. Learning the language (if it's different from yours) and learning about the culture of your new home should be a priority.

Learning the language of the country you will be living in is an obvious necessity. The more you learn of the language, the more you will feel at home. Americans are in the enviable position of being native speakers of what has become the global language of business. Because of this, many Americans do not speak any other language, so the burden of communication falls heavily on the newcomer. How well you speak English can affect people's perception of you and your ability. Make it a point to go beyond the basics of the language and delve into the intricacies as well. Learn idioms and slang, American sayings, and catch phrases.

Just as important as learning the language of your new country is learning about its culture and peoples. What are the values that the people hold, what is their history, what are their beliefs, customs, and traditions? In the "Background" section of this book, we've provided you with enough of this kind of information to whet your appetite. Don't stop there, though! There are lots of ways to go about learning the culture of your new country, including reading books and articles, talking to other expatriates or people from the country, and participating in a pre-departure (or post-arrival!) cultural orientation. Don't expect to learn everything there is to learn about the country in such a short time, or imagine that you will be prepared for every contingency; your goal is to learn enough to be comfortable in your new home. Once you arrive, you will discover on your own much more than you can ever learn from a book or from talking to other people.

Perhaps the first step in learning about your new culture is to learn about yourself and your own culture. Because culture is such an innate part of who we are, few people take the time to ponder what it is that makes them tick. Spend some time reflecting on your own cultural heritage, and ask yourself the same questions you would ask of another culture: What are *your* values? What is *your* history? What are *your* beliefs, customs, and traditions? The more you understand about yourself, the easier it will be for you to recognize cultural differences and reduce the likelihood of cultural misunderstandings.

MOVING ABROAD "DOS & DON'TS"

DO . . .

. . . have realistic expectations
. . . find out as much as you can before you go
. . . learn the language—or at least basic phrases
. . . be open-minded
. . . find several mentors and cultural guides
. . . make plans now for keeping in touch
. . . take the initiative and reach out

DON'T . . .

. . . lose touch with family and friends
. . . wait until it is time to return to plan for your repatriation
. . . wait for other people to come to you

FOUR

GETTING AROUND

Whether you're visiting the United States for a short time or living there for an extended period, you will need to be able to get from point A to point B. This chapter provides simple tips and practical information to help you get around locally and travel from city to city.

GETTING AROUND LOCALLY

With the exception of a few metropolitan areas with extensive public transportation systems, most Americans rely on their cars to get to and from work, to run errands, and so on. You, too, will rely greatly on an automobile if you live in a smaller town. However, you may live in a city with buses or subways, and sooner or later, virtually everyone will need the services of a taxi.

Driving

Most Americans own vehicles and enjoy the freedom that they provide. In fact, most people feel that they could not get along without them. Many families own two or more vehicles. Vehicle ownership starts at an early age; teenagers begin badgering their parents for a car of their own long before they receive their driver's license. Of course, not every teenager owns a car, but some parents do get their children a car, and many teens work so they can buy a car themselves.

It is important to note that the requirements and procedures for obtaining a driver's license and automobile insurance, not to mention driving laws, vary considerably from state to state. The following paragraphs should be considered as only a general overview. Information specific to your state can be obtained from the state's Department of Motor Vehicles.

The driving age differs from state to state, ranging from 15 to 18 years of age. In most states, teens can obtain a learner's permit one year before they reach the legal driving age, allowing them to drive when there is a licensed driver—in some states the teen's parent or guardian—in the vehicle with them. Once they reach driving age, they must pass a written test, a practical driving test, and a simple vision test. Driver education courses are available at some schools, and there are many driving schools for private lessons. However, in many states it is not necessary to have formal driving instruction prior to getting your license.

Automobile insurance is mandatory in all states, although the level of insurance varies. Most states require a minimum amount of liability insurance to cover damage you do to others. In addition, you can get additional liability coverage, collision coverage for damage to your own vehicle if it collides with another object, (such as a lamppost or wall), and medical insurance to cover the cost of medical treatment for injuries received in an accident. It's important to speak with a licensed automobile insurance broker who can tell you the minimum requirements for your state and advise you on additional insurance.

Like clothing fashions, car trends change with the times. Over the past few decades, American's tastes in cars have moved from large, gas-guzzling, American-made autos to small, efficient Asian-made cars, and have returned to a preference for giant, inefficient cars, such as the sport-utility vehicle (SUV). As you drive across America, you will see many of these large vehicles in cities as well as on country roads.

Rising gas prices seem to do little to discourage Americans from driving their cars. No matter what the price, Americans continue to flock to the beaches, mountains, and everywhere in between for their vacations and on holidays. Americans use their cars for everyday errands as well. Trips to the grocery store, dry cleaners, and library are made by car, even when the distance is relatively short and within walking—or biking—distance. Even in New York City, where there is an extensive public transportation system, the streets are usually packed with cars. Other cities, such as Los Angeles, don't have an adequate public transportation system, forcing residents to spend a great deal of time in their cars, trying to get from here to there. In fact, rumor has it that some Los Angelenos are so used to driving everywhere, they even drive to their next-door neighbor's house to borrow a cup of sugar!

Rules of the Road

Driving laws are set by each state individually; some cities impose other laws as well (for example, it is illegal to make a right turn at a red light in New York City). However, the federal government influences the states' laws by withholding federal funds for highway improvements if the state does not implement certain laws, such as specified speed limits. Nevertheless, there are many rules that are consistent across the country. You can contact your state's Department of Motor Vehicles for a driving manual that outlines the specific laws in your state. (You can find a telephone number in your phone book or look online. The U.S. Department of Transportation Web site, **www.dot. gov**, has links to the relevant agencies in each state. You can also visit the state's official Web site at **www.state.[state abbreviation].us**; i.e., **www.state.ny.us** for New York or **www.state.fl.us** for Florida.)

You will also want to become familiar with American road signs, which are often different from recognized international signs. Fortunately, road signs within the states are consistent. If you get a driver's manual from one of the sources listed above, it will have illustrations of the various road signs. You can also find this information online at many state Web sites.

If you are going to be traveling in other states, it is important to note that you must comply with those states' laws as well. For example, if your state does not require passengers to wear a seatbelt, but you travel through a state that does, everyone has to buckle up! (Of course, safety belt laws are there to ensure the safety of everyone, so it's a good idea for everyone in the car to wear a safety belt at all times, even if it hasn't been legislated in your area.)

All roads have posted speed limits, although the maximum speed limit varies from state to state. In general, speed limits in and around cities range from 15–50 miles per hour, while the limits on highways can be as high as 70–80 mph. If you are stopped for speeding, be prepared to show your driver's license, vehicle registration, and proof of insurance. If you want to pay for the ticket immediately, you will probably have to follow the officer to the local city hall; otherwise, you can mail a check to pay for the ticket.

A point system is used by most states to track violations. Points added to your driving record can result in increased insurance premiums. Too many points will result in your driver's license being suspended.

Wearing a seatbelt is mandatory for the driver and passengers in the front of the vehicle in every state but New Hampshire. In 13 states and in the District of Columbia, seat belt laws apply to passengers in the vehicle's back seat as well. In most states, you cannot be stopped for not wearing your seatbelt, but you will receive an additional fine if you are stopped for another reason, such as speeding, and are not wearing a seatbelt. (Note that many states are currently attempting to pass legislation that will allow the police to stop drivers for not wearing a seatbelt.)

All states have child restraint laws, which require that children under a specified age be placed in approved safety seats. The age at which a child can wear an adult seatbelt varies. If you have children, you will want to carefully check the laws in your area.

Helmet laws for motorcyclists vary and are quite complicated, so if you ride, you will need to verify your local laws. A handful of states don't require the use of helmets, but most have some laws in place, especially for younger riders; some also require additional insurance. Be sure to check the laws of not only your state, but any state where you will be biking.

Many street intersections are four-way stops. That is, there is a stop sign for vehicles coming from all directions. At these intersections, the car that arrives first should be allowed to proceed while other vehicles wait. If two or more cars arrive simultaneously, the vehicle on the right has the right of way unless there is a sign stating otherwise.

Pedestrians should be given the right of way whenever possible. However, many drivers do not stop at pedestrian crosswalks. When you stop for pedestrians, be sure that traffic behind you isn't too close to stop.

Although the left lane is supposed to be for passing only, most people tend to ignore this and drive in all lanes. Many larger cities have lanes that are designed to encourage people to carpool with others instead of driving their individual vehicles. These lanes are often called HOV (High Occupancy Vehicle) lanes and are marked with a diamond. Signs will indicate their presence and the rules, such as the number of people you must have in the vehicle in order to use the lane and the hours the lane is for restricted use.

If you are in an automobile accident, you will want to notify the police, since your insurance company will require a police report in order to pay your claim. Exchange the following information with anyone else involved: vehicle license number, driver's name and address, and driver's insurance company. You may also want to get the names and addresses of any witnesses. Talk to your insurance agent about the proper procedures for making an insurance claim if you are involved in an accident.

The United States has recently seen two trends that have resulted in an alarming increase in automobile accidents: "road rage" and cellular phone use.

The number of vehicles on the road has outgrown the infrastructure in many places, resulting in terrible traffic and frustrated motorists. Unfortunately, frustration sometimes turns into "road rage." In lesser cases, this can be cursing and offensive gesturing. However, it can also escalate into retaliatory moves, such as speeding up and cutting in front of someone who cut in front of you, or even bumping that person's car. In the worst cases, this type of reckless driving has resulted in fatal accidents, and enraged drivers have even pulled out guns and shot the perceived offender.

Most Americans spend a lot of time in their cars and they are usually in a hurry. In order to make their drives a more efficient use of their time, many people have begun taking their cellular phones with them so they can make calls while they drive. Drivers using a cellular phone without a headset have only one hand on the wheel and their eyes aren't always on the road. Even when a headset is used, however, the driver is distracted. Cellular phones are not the only culprit; computerized guidance systems are appearing in more and more vehicles and cause similar distractions. To date, a handful of states have made it illegal to use a phone, with or without a headset, while driving. In other areas, it's always a good idea to steer clear of drivers who are talking on the phone. If you have a cell phone and need to make a call, the safest thing to do is to pull off the road so you don't endanger yourself or others by being distracted while driving.

Public Transportation

Subways, Trams, and Commuter Trains

Several major cities, including New York, Atlanta, Boston, Washington, D.C., San Francisco, and Chicago, have extensive underground and aboveground rail systems. Each city operates its own transportation

system, making it difficult to find across-the-board similarities. Your fare may allow you to travel the entire system or the amount you pay may be based on the distance you are traveling. For some, you need to purchase a token or fare card, for others, you can pay with cash. In fact, many offer multiple payment methods. In most cases, you will pay before going through turnstiles to access the tracks. The station may have a manned ticket or token booth, or you may be able to buy the token or ticket from a machine.

Navigating your way through an unfamiliar subway system can be overwhelming and confusing, so be sure to leave plenty of time for your trip until you become familiar with how things work. A map of the system is usually posted at every stop and in the cars themselves. You can also obtain a map at a token booth, on the Web site of the transportation authority that operates the system, or on the city's visitors bureau Web site. Web sites can also provide information on prices and ways to save money, such as multiple trip discounts. If you're going to be using the train to commute to and from work every day, you will probably be able to get a flat-rate pass that will allow you unlimited trips during the month, or similar savings.

Tips for a Smooth Ride

- Some local transportation stops running overnight. Be sure to check to see when the last bus or train leaves or you will have to return by taxi, which can be expensive.
- There is an unwritten rule that the boundaries of personal space should be respected. Of course, on a crowded rush hour subway train, passengers are packed together, so it's difficult not to bump into people. However, you will notice that people entering an empty train or bus will attempt to keep an empty seat between themselves and the other passengers until the vehicle fills up too much to make this feasible. Therefore, you will probably be viewed suspiciously if you sit right next to someone on an empty train, or if you sit next to someone on the bus when there is an empty row available.
- When on the subway, train, or bus, it is considered polite to yield your seat to the elderly, the disabled, pregnant women, or parents traveling with small children. Unfortunately, though, this doesn't always happen.

Buses

Buses can provide an economical way to get around, but few cities have well-developed bus systems. On most buses, you will pay with cash—bills or coins—but you must have the exact fare; bus drivers are usually not able to give you change. Commuters can buy a monthly pass. You will enter the bus at the front and put your money in the slot; you can exit from the front or the back. Buses generally stop only when there is someone waiting at the stop or when someone on board signals for a stop, usually by pressing a button or strip to alert the driver. If you are unsure which stop you want, upon boarding you can ask the driver to let you know when you get there.

Buses can be operated by the city, private companies, or both. Most cities have a main bus terminal where you can get information on bus routes and schedules; the bus driver can tell you the fare.

Taxis and Car Service

In larger cities, taxis can be hailed on the street or found at taxi stands in front of hotels, airports, theaters, and other places. If you want to make arrangements in advance, or if you live in a smaller town, you can call to have a taxi come pick you up. The telephone numbers can be found in the yellow pages of your phone book (look under "taxicabs"). If you need transportation for a lot of people, many taxi companies offer minivan service.

Taxi fares should be posted in the car; many times they are painted on the outside of the vehicle. Once you get in the taxi, the driver should start the meter; if he or she does not, you can ask that the meter be used. Although the driver should be able to give you change, it's usually best to carry small bills. It's customary to tip the driver 15–20%, though if the trip is a short one, most people tip more, adding $1–$4.

Sometimes the taxi driver will try to take two fares at once to maximize the amount of money that he or she can earn. If you are not comfortable sharing a ride with someone you don't know, you do not have to, and the driver cannot insist. If you want to make a complaint against the driver for this, or any other reason, you should write down the driver's name and/or taxi number. The phone number of the city's taxi commission should be posted in the taxi, or it can be found in the telephone book.

The quality of taxi service can vary drastically. Taxi drivers, especially those in large cities, have a reputation for being reckless drivers and the condition of the vehicle is often questionable. It's a good idea to speak to colleagues or friends, or to the local visitor's bureau, to find out if there are any safety tips you should be aware of. For example, taxis usually need to be licensed, but unlicensed "gypsy" taxicabs often try to pick up fares as well. Gypsy cabs are not well-regulated, and therefore could be more costly or possibly unsafe. You should learn the signs for identifying a licensed taxi, such as the medallions mounted on the hoods of New York's yellow-painted cabs.

An alternative to taxis is livery or car service. Livery and car service vehicles are usually nicer than taxis. They are often Lincoln Town Cars or other luxury vehicles, and because they are usually owned by the driver, they are usually well maintained. Companies often use car services when employees need to get to the airport or to give them a safe ride home when they work late. They can be hired to provide a comfortable ride at rates that are usually competitive with taxi rates.

GETTING FROM CITY TO CITY

America's love affair with the automobile definitely extends to intercity travel. Most middle-class Americans remember—fondly or otherwise—at least one vacation when the family piled into the car and drove to visit Grandma or the Grand Canyon, with the kids fighting in the back seat and driving Mom and Dad crazy by constantly asking "Are we there yet?" The idea of a road trip anticipates the feeling of freedom that driving brings, of speeding toward a destination or meandering through scenic back roads with no particular destination in mind.

Renting a Car

Renting a car is a simple matter if you have a credit card and a driver's license. You can make a reservation by telephone or online at one of many national car rental agencies (Avis, Budget, Dollar, Hertz, and National are some of the best-known names). You will need to give your credit card number to make the reservation, but you can cancel the reservation at any time and your card will not be charged until you pick up the rented car. Note, though, that most states have an age requirement for renting cars; in most places you have to be 21 to rent a car, but in some, the age restriction is as high as 25. If you fall beneath one of those age categories, you may find that you must pay a higher rental rate for insurance reasons.

Car rental pickup locations can be found at most airports and in other locations in major cities; some companies will even deliver the car to you. When you pick up the car, you will have the option of returning it with the gas tank full or empty; if you choose the latter, a full tank of gas will be added to your bill, usually at higher rates than those found at local gas stations. You will also have the option to buy insurance for the car. Damage to a rental car will often be covered by your own automobile insurance (if you have a car), but you might find that your insurance coverage is inadequate to cover damage to a new rental car. Talk to your insurance provider for advice before deciding about additional insurance for a rental car.

Planes

Driving across the United States can take a week, so a quicker method of transportation is sometimes necessary. There are many national and regional airlines that will get you where you want to go quickly, although not always cheaply.

American, Continental, Delta, and US Airways are some of the major national (and international) airlines; Southwest and Northwest are two examples of regional airlines. Of course, there are many smaller airlines to choose from as well. Each of the major airlines has at least one—and sometimes more than one—major hub city, which can make one airline more or less convenient for you.

There are many ways to buy an airline ticket. You can visit a travel agent, who can go over all of your travel options as well as arrange for other travel needs, such as a rental car or a hotel. If you prefer to do it yourself, you can call the airlines directly for schedule and fare information. Or you can look online, either on the airline's Web site or a site that can book on any airline, such as Expedia.com or Travelocity.com.

When you find a fare you like, you can make a reservation that is valid for 24 hours. However, the reservation just guarantees the seat, not the fare; if the fare changes in that time period, you must pay the new fare. If you do not pay for the ticket within the 24-hour period, your reservation will be automatically canceled.

When you get to the airport, you can check in at the airline's counter or outside at the airline's curbside check-in location. If you don't have any luggage to check, you can go directly to the flight's gate and check in there. If you check in with a skycap or have a porter help you with your luggage, it's customary to tip him or her about $1 per bag.

E-tickets (electronic tickets) are becoming more and more popular as a way to streamline the check-in process. If you purchased an e-ticket, you simply insert your frequent flier card or a credit card into one of the machines located in the check-in or gate area.

No matter where you check in, you will be asked a couple of security questions, such as Did you pack your own luggage? or Has anyone asked you to carry something on board?

After the events of September 11, 2001, the U.S. government implemented new airport security measures. Airport security was handed over to the Transportation Security Administration, a federal government organization working to unify airport security measures across the United States. Currently, only ticketed passengers are allowed at the gate; family and friends meeting loved ones or seeing them off must wait in the main terminal. You will go through a metal detector on your way to the gate, and your carry-on luggage will be X-rayed. Airport employees can ask to search your luggage, remove your shoes, or search your person if they find anything to be suspicious. Airports also have dogs trained to detect drugs and bombs. It is important to note that in the United States, it is illegal to mention bombs in an airport, even as a joke. Such comments are taken very seriously: at the very least, you will be taken aside for questioning and a search. Other threats and violations of security are taken very seriously in airports, and have been the reason behind several airport shutdowns. To make sure you are kept up-to-date with airport security measures, you can check the Security Tips for Air Travelers on the FAA (Federal Aviation Administration) Web site (**www.faa.gov**).

Trains

Train travel has largely been replaced by airplane travel. However, some routes remain popular, such as the routes between Washington, D.C., New York City and Boston. Trains offer the benefit of stations conveniently located in the downtown area, eliminating the need for a harried, and often expensive, taxi ride to the airport.

While most major cities have trains that offer commuter service to nearby suburbs, the only national intercity train service is offered by Amtrak. Find schedule and fare information and purchase tickets by telephone (1-800-USA-RAIL) or online at **www.amtrak.com**.

Buses

Intercity buses offer the most economical, but often the slowest, trip between cities. Greyhound and Trailways are the two companies that offer nationwide bus service; many other companies offer regional service. When you are ready to schedule your bus trip, check your local yellow pages to find out what buses serve your area; information can also be found on the Internet. Buses usually stop in all cities, major and minor, along the route. The buses themselves can be quite comfortable, and they will have a bathroom on board.

BICYCLE RIDERS AND PEDESTRIANS

Americans ride bikes more for pleasure and exercise than they do for everyday transportation. There are a few basic rules you need to be aware of when you pull out your bicycle. Bicycle riders are subject to the same rules as cars—that is, you should bike with the flow of traffic, not against it, and obey traffic lights and street signs. Cyclists should signal turns and stops. Raise your left hand straight out to indicate a left turn; bend your elbow and point your hand up to signal a right turn (some cyclists hold their right arm straight out to indicate a right turn). To signal a stop, hold your left arm out, bent at the elbow with your hand pointing down. Cyclists will find few bicycle lanes, and those that exist are often treated as an extended sidewalk by pedestrians. In large cities, you will see cyclists who seem to feel that these rules do not apply to them. However, breaking these rules can result in being ticketed by the police; in fact, many cities have recently begun to enforce biking laws more strictly in an attempt to prevent accidents between bicycles and vehicles.

Pedestrians should walk on the sidewalk on either side of the street. If you are on a road that does not have a sidewalk, be sure you walk on the side facing traffic; you don't want your back to oncoming cars. Many city street corners have walk/don't walk signals, but pedestrians often tend to be too impatient to wait, and ignore them. Crossing against the light is illegal, as is jaywalking, or crossing the street in the middle of the block rather than at the corner. It is possible to get a ticket for these actions.

SAFETY

Safety is a concern for all travelers, whether they are going to work or visiting a new city. Unfortunately, muggings and carjackings are not unheard of in the United States. As is true when you travel anywhere, being alert is your best defense. Follow the same rules that apply whenever you are in an unfamiliar place: keep a careful watch on your purse or wallet, don't flash money or expensive jewelry, don't carry a lot of money, and keep a copy of important documents separate from the documents themselves.

Home burglaries also occur in the United States. If you are going on a trip, there are several things you can do to keep your home from being a target for burglars. For example, tell your neighbors that you are going away so they can keep an eye out for intruders. Ask a neighbor to pick up your mail and newspaper; an overflowing mailbox and a week's worth of newspapers is a sure sign that the homeowner is away. You can also purchase inexpensive timers at your local hardware store that will automatically turn your lights on for a few hours each night, giving the illusion that you are home. Many neighborhoods also have a Neighborhood Watch program that encourages everyone in the neighborhood to notice and report anyone who is acting suspiciously or who does not belong in the neighborhood.

If you would like to learn more about being safe in your neighborhood, you can contact your local police department; use the non-emergency number listed in your phone book's blue pages. Most police departments have programs for the community that you can take advantage of, such as self-defense classes and assistance setting up a Neighborhood Watch program where you live.

IN AN EMERGENCY

If you have an emergency, you can get help by dialing 911[1]. The 911 operator will need to know the nature of your emergency, so he or she can send the police, fire department, or ambulance, as well as the address you are calling from. The 911 operator is also trained to assist you in providing basic emergency care until help arrives. Unless you are in imminent danger, such as your home being on fire, you should stay on the line with the operator until help arrives.

[1]Note: while 911 is the standard emergency number for the U.S., there are a handful of rural areas where this service is not available. Check your local telephone book to verify that 911 is valid where you live; if it is not, keep the phone numbers for the local police, fire, and ambulance services next to your phone.

In areas where there are many people who do not speak English, the 911 service may have bilingual operators; the second language is usually Spanish. In most cases, however, the 911 operator will speak English only, so it is important that every family member know a few basic phrases in English to be able to summon the appropriate type of help.

It is a good idea to familiarize yourself with the insurance procedures you need to follow in a medical emergency to ensure that your medical bills will be covered. For example, in a life-threatening situation, such as a heart attack or stroke, your insurance will probably cover you for medical attention at the nearest hospital. However, when your life is not in danger, such as when you break your leg, your insurance provider may require that the injury be treated at a member hospital or that you call to get clearance before being admitted. Find out what steps you will need to take in case of an emergency as soon as you get insurance; don't wait until the emergency happens.

FIVE

LIVING AND STAYING IN THE UNITED STATES

HOUSING

Housing is perhaps the biggest and most immediate concern for anyone moving. When you move to the United States, you will have several
decisions to make.

Things to Consider

When you are searching for your new home, you will want to be sure it
fits your needs as closely as possible. The most obvious consideration is
the cost, but you should think about the following as well.

How will you (or your spouse) get to work? Few cities in the United
States have good public transportation systems. In fact, most Americans drive their cars to work. In some parts of the country, particularly
near major cities such as New York, Los Angeles, or Chicago, people
commute up to two hours each way to and from work. Decide how far
away from work you are willing to live and how long of a commute you
are willing to make. And if you are moving with a spouse or partner,
how will he or she get around if you take the car to work?

Do you have children with schooling needs? If you do, you want them to get the best possible education. You will need to research the schools that will be available to them and plan how they will get there and back. Your decision on where to live may hinge on what school you want your children to attend.

Types of Homes

Homes in America are as diverse as the people. From the brownstones of New York City to the ranch houses of Texas, every area has its own look and feel. Here are some of the different types of homes available:

Detached house, single-family or ranch. A detached house is a one-family home with its own grounds, large or small. Although you may not find many detached houses in the downtown areas of large cities, they abound in suburbs across America. They may simply be in a neighborhood, or they can be part of a housing complex, often a

gated community that provides a measure of security and a friendly atmosphere. The style of the houses available depends on the area.

Semi-detached house or duplex. Semi-detached homes share a common wall, but have a yard around the building. These are common in more populated areas and fall somewhere between a free-standing home and an apartment building.

Townhouse. Townhouses are rows of homes, usually two or more stories, which are attached on the sides. Townhouses are usually part of a housing complex, and can be rented or purchased. Purchasing a townhouse offers the benefits of home ownership with fewer responsibilities, since tasks such as grounds maintenance, snow removal, etc. are taken care of by the management company.

Apartment. The term apartment covers everything from towering buildings to a house that has been converted into smaller units. A "walk-up" is an apartment in a building with no elevator—you have to walk up the stairs to your apartment. A "studio" refers to an apartment that is one area; there are no walls to delineate the bedroom, living room, etc. A "loft" refers to a converted industrial building with large open spaces; the renter is usually responsible for modifying the interiors to suit their needs.

Condominium (Condo). Condominium refers to individual ownership of an apartment in a multi-unit structure. Like a townhouse, if you purchase a condominium, you will pay your mortgage plus an additional monthly fee to the condominium association. This fee covers communal costs, such as grounds maintenance. The term "condo" is also often used to describe a spacious, usually luxurious, apartment that one can rent for a limited time; this is a popular alternative to a hotel for many vacationers.

What to Expect

Although you can find furnished apartments, unfurnished apartments and houses are the norm. However, an unfurnished place in the United States includes much more than similar homes in other countries. A typical unfurnished apartment will have kitchen appliances, although the kind of appliances can vary. An oven/stove and kitchen cabinetry are standard, and a refrigerator is usually included. Appliances you may or may not find are a microwave, dishwasher, and clothes washer/dryer. You will have some way to heat your apartment, but you may need to purchase an air-conditioner. Your ceiling lights will be there, but you will need to provide lamps or other lighting. Many newcomers to the United States are astonished at the size of closets in their new home. While some homes do have limited closet space, many homes, especially newer ones, have enormous walk-in closets.

If you do rent a furnished apartment, it will include basic furniture in the living room—such as a couch, chairs, and tables—a dining room table and chairs, beds and a chest of drawers in the bedroom, as well as lamps and other lighting throughout the house. Items like bed linens and kitchen utensils are included only in corporate apartments, which are for short-term stays.

You will probably be expected to fill out a rental application and sign a lease when you rent an apartment. The term of the lease varies, but most are for one year. The landlord or rental agent may check your credit history. Because your rental or credit history is in another country, it will not show up on a credit report. It can help if you bring a statement of payment history from your previous landlord or from the bank that held your mortgage if you owned your home. A letter from your employer confirming your employment there can also help.

When you rent an apartment, you will have to pay a deposit and possibly make other payments. For example, a common policy is to require a security deposit equal to the monthly rent, plus the first and last month's rent. This is a guarantee that the tenant will not leave without paying the rent. Therefore, if your monthly rent is $500, you will need to write a check for $1,500. Of course, you will not have to pay your last month's rent when you move, since you will have paid it in your first check. Your deposit and any other security money should be held in an interest-bearing escrow account.

In most cases, you will need to notify your landlord at least 30 days before you move out of your apartment. If you do not, you must pay the following month's rent. If you decide to move before the term of your lease ends, you may be responsible for paying the remainder of the lease. However, if the landlord is able to find another tenant quickly, you may not have to pay the entire amount. When you move out of an apartment, you are entitled to reclaim your deposit, although the landlord can deduct the expense of cleaning the apartment or repairing any damage you caused.

Finding a Living Space

There are many ways to find a home. If you are considering buying your own home, you will probably want to work with a real estate broker (also called a real estate agent) to find a home that meets your needs. If you are looking for a house or an apartment to rent, you can also find a real estate broker, or you can check the classified advertising section in the local newspaper. If you are moving to a large city, you may be able to view ads on the Internet as well. Some areas have large apartment complexes that are managed by a property management company; if you see one that looks suitable, you can visit the management office, which is usually located on the premises, to ask if there are any apartments available.

Obviously, it will be difficult to find housing before you arrive. Many people spend several weeks at a hotel when they first arrive while they seek housing. While this is certainly one alternative, you can also try to find a semi-permanent home from abroad. For example, you could ask American colleagues or the human resources department of your organization for referrals to a local broker or property management company. If you provide the broker with your minimum requirements (number of bedrooms, monthly rental budget, distance from work, etc.), he or she can look for an apartment that can be rented or leased for three to six months. This will give you a home base while you explore your new city and decide where you want to live. Another alternative is to locate a company that places incoming expatriates in temporary, furnished housing on a weekly or monthly basis.

If you prefer to work with a real estate agent (or an apartment search company if you are looking to rent), you can locate one by asking colleagues or friends for recommendations. You can also check in the yellow pages to find a local agent or check for ads in the newspaper. When you select an agent, you will want to make sure he or she is licensed. You can also check with the local Better Business Bureau (BBB—you'll find an address and a telephone number in the phone book) to see if there have been any complaints against the company. In almost every case, the real estate agent's fee is usually paid by the renter or buyer. Although fees vary, it is usually a percentage (4–7%) of the sale price if you are buying a house, or a percentage of one year's rent, such as 150% of your monthly rent.

Reading the Ads

Since the person who places an advertisement in a newspaper has to pay per word or character, most ads use abbreviations. Here are some of the most common ones:

Apt	Apartment
Twnhse	Townhouse
EIK	Eat-in Kitchen (a kitchen that is large enough to hold a table for dining)
BR	Bedroom (apartments and houses are listed more often by number of bedrooms—1BR, 2BR, 3BR, etc.—than by square footage)
Bath/Bth	Bathroom
Rm	Room
W/w carpet	wall-to-wall carpeting (fully carpeted)
LR	Living room
DR	Dining room
Mod	Modern

Remod	Remodeled
Bsmt or fin bsmt	Basement or finished basement (a finished basement is one that can be used as a room)
HW or hdwd flrs	Hardwood floors
Fplc	Fireplace
A/C	Air-conditioning
C/A or CAC	Central air-conditioning
D/W	Dishwasher
W/D	Clothes washer and dryer

BRINGING YOUR BELONGINGS

Of course you will want to bring the things that will make your new house or apartment feel like home. It is important, though, to think things through before you start packing. Consider the fact that your appliances and electronic equipment will need to be adapted to the American electrical voltage and plug configuration, and even then they may not work at peak performance because of the difference in Hertz values. Many people moving abroad find it preferable to leave most of their appliances at home (or sell them) and apply the money they would have spent moving them to purchasing new equipment once they arrive.

A second option is to contact a company that specializes in furnishing appliances that meet international specifications. This will allow you to purchase your appliances before leaving and arrange for their delivery to your new home, saving you the hassle of shopping in an unfamiliar environment, especially when you will probably have many other things to do to get settled.

Remember that American measurements are not based on metrics. (See Appendix C on Metric Conversions.) This will impact your life in more ways than you can imagine. For example, if you are tak-

ing your family's beds with you, you may find that sheets bought in the United States—and therefore measured in inches instead of centimeters—won't fit. You will need to take your metric-measured linens with you or be prepared to use flat sheets only. The same applies, of course, if you are bringing items purchased in the United States back with you.

Appliances and Computers

Electricity in the United States is 110 volts (60-Hertz). If your appliances operate on a 220-volt (50-Hertz) system, they will not work without a current transformer. In addition, appliances such as refrigerators, air conditioners, clocks, microwaves, vacuum cleaners, and stereos will not work properly, even with a transformer, because of the difference in Hertz.

The United States uses two types of plugs. The most common has two flat, parallel prongs. If your appliance needs to be grounded, it will have a third, round prong centered below the flat prongs. If you want to use any of your own appliances, you will probably want to have several plug adapters so you don't have to switch the adapter between appliances.

There are several options for obtaining appliances for your new home. You will first want to see what appliances, if any, come with your house or apartment. If you need other appliances, you can, of course, buy them locally. However, there are other alternatives. For example, you can look into buying them from other people who are leaving the country. If your company has a large contingent of expatriates, the human resources department may be able to put you in touch with a colleague who is leaving the United States. You can also look in a local newspaper for ads listing used appliances for sale by private individuals. There are also companies that specialize in providing appliances to people moving overseas that meet the local requirements. Some of these companies are listed in Appendix B.

There are hundreds of Internet service providers (ISPs) in the United States. Popular ISPs are AOL, Earthlink, and MSN. Basic monthly fees range from about $10 to $30; some ISPs have premium packages that cost more but offer services such as high-speed or DSL connections, multiple e-mail addresses, and so on. A little bit of research will tell you which ISPs have local connection phone numbers. If you live in a very rural area or a very small town, you may not be able to find an ISP with a local connection. In those cases, most ISPs will give you a toll-free number to use for connection; this service has an additional monthly fee. In most places, the telephone company does not charge a per-call fee for local phone calls; however, if you live in a city where there is a per-call usage fee, such as New York City, you will have to pay that fee to the telephone company each time you connect to your ISP.

Vehicles

If you want to bring your vehicle with you when you move to the United States, you will need to be sure it complies with the standards set by the United States Department of Transportation (DOT). If your vehicle does not comply with these standards, it can only be brought into the United States by an importer registered with the DOT and a bond for 150% of the value of the vehicle must be posted. The registered importer will then modify and certify your vehicle.

For more information on the forms you will need to import your vehicle and on the federal vehicle motor safety standards, you can visit the Web site of the U.S. Department of Transportation at **www.dot.gov**.

If you do import your vehicle, you will need to register it in the state where you will be living and comply with state vehicle inspection laws; contact the state's Department of Motor Vehicles (DMV—also called the Department of Public Safety and Motor Vehicles or the Office of Motor Vehicles in some states) for more information. You can look in your telephone book for the number of an office near you or online to find information.

SHOPPING

When you make your first shopping foray in the United States, you will be faced with a multitude of shopping options. You can spend an entire day browsing through the stores of a mall or you can do your shopping without ever leaving your house.

Shopping malls. The state of Minnesota boasts the Mall of America, the largest fully enclosed retail and entertainment complex in the United States with more than 520 stores and an indoor roller coaster. Although that is enormous even by American standards, these indoor shopping centers have appeared all across the country. They offer the convenience of many different types of shops and entertainment, such as movies, restaurants, and gaming arcades, in one central location.

Strip malls. A scaled-down version of shopping malls, strip malls have several stores connected together in a row or in a small enclave. A typical strip mall might have a supermarket, a drug store, and several specialty stores.

Department stores. Department stores are large stores that carry a variety of goods, such as clothing, jewelry, cosmetics, furniture, housewares, home furnishings, appliances, automotive supplies,

and more. Some department stores carry higher-priced goods than others, and some are national chains while others are regional or local. Some department stores that you might see are Sears, JCPenney, Macy's, Dillard's, and Lord & Taylor.

Discount stores/Megastores. There are several chains of large discount stores in the United States. The best-known are Wal-Mart, KMart, and Target. These stores began by offering clothing, housewares, and other items at lower prices than department stores. However, most have expanded to include food, pharmaceuticals, and many other items, offering one-stop shopping.

Specialty stores. Everywhere you go, you will find many stores or boutiques that specialize in certain items. This might be anything from lingerie stores to hobby shops to bait-and-tackle stores. No matter what you are looking for, you are likely to find that somewhere in the United States there is a store specializing in it!

Convenience stores. Most convenience stores are open 24 hours a day and have a small amount of a variety products such as groceries, candy, newspapers, and automotive goods; many are also part of gas stations. If you find yourself in need of milk in the middle of the night, or if you are just having a craving for ice cream, a convenience store is the place to go.

Drug stores. Drug stores in the United States are not just apothecaries; in addition to prescription and over-the-counter (non-prescription) medication, most drug stores carry a little bit of everything: health and beauty supplies, school supplies, toys, and even food.

Catalog or online shopping. The Internet has opened up new vistas in shopping. You can now purchase virtually everything, from books, to clothes, to a house, online. If you have a favorite store, they probably have a Web site where you can get information about their products and often even order items to be delivered to your door. Many Americans take advantage of the convenience offered by online shopping, especially when it's time to give gifts, such as Christmas or Mother's Day.

Food Shopping

Unlike shopping for household items or clothing, you may actually find that you have fewer options when it comes to buying food. Specialty shops, such as the butcher or the baker, are very difficult to find and simply do not exist in many places. Even smaller grocery stores (called "Mom & Pop" stores) are vanishing, as large supermarkets and megastores take over. You will find the parking lots of these large stores full as people go on their biweekly or monthly shopping trips, stocking their freezers and refrigerators for the coming weeks.

Convenience is the hallmark of modern America, and the stores are laden with products to make life easier. If the container says "instant" or "quick," you can bet Americans will buy it! Many American families regularly use frozen foods, such as frozen vegetables, pizza, and even entire frozen meals called TV dinners (they get their name from what many people do while they eat these meals). Many other products lure busy people with the promise of a nutritious meal in minutes.

Supermarkets. Supermarkets offer the convenience of doing all of your food shopping in one place. You will find a wide variety of types of food and brands in your local supermarket. Many have an in-store bakery and delicatessen along with other specialty sections, such as gourmet foods, wine and liquor, or frozen food. Supermarkets also carry non-food items, such as health and beauty products, cleaning products, school supplies, etc. Many also have pharmacies, so you can drop off a prescription when you arrive, carry on with your shopping, and pick it up when you leave.

Warehouses/Wholesale stores. Recent trends in shopping are warehouse or wholesale stores. These stores offer a wide variety of goods at low prices. Some, such as BJ's or Sam's, have food and household items; others, such as Costco, carry electronics, furniture, etc. Especially in warehouses that carry food, the quantities are very large; families are most likely to find this a good shopping alternative.

Many of these stores require you to become a member and charge a modest annual membership fee. The idea, of course, is that the amount you will save by buying at wholesale prices will outweigh the annual fee. However, if you would like to visit a store to see if you are interested, most membership clubs will allow you to shop one time at no charge or for a small fee.

Sales Tax

When you make your purchases, don't forget that sales tax is not included in most products and services. The sales tax can be set by the state, county, city, or a combination of these. In most places, the sales tax is within the range of 6%–8.5%. Some places and services, such as those linked to tourism, have higher taxes. You will find some areas that have special economic zones where sales tax is as low as 3%, and in some areas certain items are not taxed at all.

Returns

As stores compete for sales, emphasis is placed on customer service as a way to lure and keep customers, and American consumers place a great deal of importance on convenience. The combination of these factors means that virtually everything you buy is returnable. You can, of course, return an item that is defective, but you can also return it simply because you changed your mind. If you decide that the fuchsia blouse simply does not match the pattern in your skirt, or if your wife does not care for the scarf you bought her, it can be returned. Stores have varying policies on returns, so check before you buy. For example, clothing may need to have the tags still attached or items may need to be in their original packaging. You will need to have the purchase receipt and there may be a limited time during which you can make an exchange or return. Some stores will accept a return, but will issue you store credit instead of a refund.

Saving Money

Many frugal Americans use coupons for a multitude of goods and services. You will see coupons for everything from food to clothing to an oil change for your car. These coupons give you a certain amount off the price of the goods or services you are buying. You will see coupons in the Sunday newspaper, and you are sure to receive promotional mail containing coupons. Coupons and lists of sale items can also be found at the front of many stores.

Sales are frequent events in America. Virtually every holiday offers the opportunity for a sale, even when there is no connection between the holiday and the items for sale. For example, near Presidents' Day, your local electronics store will probably have a sale on everything from computers to cellular phones. Holidays aren't the only time you'll find sales, though. Many stores, especially large national or regional chain stores, have weekly sales. If you look in your Sunday paper, you are sure to find advertisements and circulars that show what items will be on sale in the coming week. If you have a purchase to make and you do not need the item right away, it will probably go on sale sooner or later; you can often save a lot of money if you can wait for a sale, especially if the item is expensive.

Other Shopping Notes

When you first go shopping in another country, there are many details that will seem odd to you. The following tips will help familiarize you with how Americans shop.

In most stores, the cashier will pack your groceries; in some stores, you may be able to select a checkout lane where you can bag your own groceries if you prefer to do so. A few stores even offer self-service checkout lanes where you scan the items yourself and put your credit or debit card into a machine to pay.

You may be offered a choice of paper or plastic bags; there is no extra charge for the bags. However, most Americans use plastic bags, so paper bags may be hard to find. Few Americans bring a bag or bags with them when they shop. In fact, most Americans shop infrequently, so their shopping carts are often overflowing by the time they get to the cashier. They would need dozens of bags to hold all of their groceries. So, despite the waste, most people get new bags when they shop; these bags are reused at home or simply thrown away. Some stores have bins where you can bring used shopping bags for recycling. However, if you prefer to take your own shopping bags when you shop, please feel free to do so!

Some stores employ people who will bag your groceries and take them out to your car for you. Even if the store where you are shopping does not have someone ready to help you after you pay for your groceries, you can get assistance with your purchases by asking the cashier to call someone to help you. When someone helps you with your groceries, it is not necessary to tip that person, although some people do slip him or her some coins or a dollar or two. You can observe other customers to see what they do.

No matter what you are buying, you will usually have several options to pay for your purchases. Virtually every store, from discount stores to pricey boutiques, accepts cash, checks, credit cards, or debit cards. If you want to write a check, you will need to provide at least one piece of identification with your picture on it (i.e., your U.S. driver's license or your passport). As a precaution, some stores may not be willing to accept starter checks; you may wish to inquire before making your purchase. Starter checks are the checks you get from the bank when you open an account; they do not have your name or address printed on them and are for you to use temporarily until your personalized checks arrive.

WEIGHTS, MEASURES, AND THE LIKE

The metric system is not used in the United States. If you are from a country that uses metrics, you will have to adjust to reading the temperature in Fahrenheit, distances in miles, and buying meat in pounds. (See Appendix C, Metric Conversions, for more information.)

American clothing and shoe sizes are very different from many other countries. As is usually the case, it's best to try a variety of items to get an idea of the sizes that best fit you. Appendix C has a chart for converting common clothing and shoe sizes.

GETTING A SOCIAL SECURITY NUMBER

One of the first things anyone who comes to United States to work needs is a Social Security number. This nine-digit number allows the government to track your contributions to the country's Social Security system. Your employer will need your Social Security number so that the proper deductions can be taken from your paycheck.

Social Security numbers are also used as personal identification numbers in many instances. For example, when you apply for a credit card, open a bank account, or request a telephone number, you will be asked for your Social Security number. If the company needs to check your credit history, they will do so using your Social Security number. The number may also become your account number or used as a way to identify you when you call for customer service. Because you will use your Social Security number frequently, it's a good idea to memorize it.

You cannot apply for a Social Security before you arrive in the United States because your visa only permits you to travel to the United States to apply for entry. When you arrive and are admitted, you will receive documentation of your admission into the country and your work authorization status. Once you have received those documents, you can apply for a Social Security card. To apply, you will need to complete the appropriate application form, which can be obtained from any Social Security Administration office or downloaded from their Web site at **www.ssa.gov**. You will also need to submit documents showing your age, identity, and lawful alien status. All of these documents must be in the original form; duplicates or notarized copies are not accepted. You can take all of your paperwork into a Social Security office or you can mail the documents to them; however, since originals are required, it may be preferable to go to the office in person to ensure that none of your papers gets misplaced.

Information on all aspects of the application process, including acceptable forms of identification and office locations, can be obtained by calling the SSA toll-free at 1-800-772-1213 or visiting their Web site at **www.ssa.gov**.

UTILITIES AND TELEPHONE SERVICE

Starting Service

You will want to make arrangements for telephone and utilities services as soon as you know where you will be living. Your first step, of course, will be to find out who your local service providers are. All telephone and utility services are provided by private companies. Depending on where you live, you may have a choice of service providers. You can find out who your local service providers are by asking friends or coworkers, your real estate broker, or by looking in the telephone book.

Starting service in your new home is as simple as making a telephone call or two to get the services put in your name. If you are moving into a newly built home or into a home whose previous tenants had service discontinued, it may take a little longer to get service started or restarted, but the process is still the same.

You may be required to make a deposit, especially if you do not have a credit history in the United States. This amount is usually relatively small ($25–$35), and will be refunded after one year if you pay your bills on time or when you change service providers. It is important to note that if you are required to make a deposit, your service will not be started until the deposit is received. For this reason, most telephone and utility companies suggest calling a few weeks before your move to ensure that your service is available when you move into your new home. However, if you are not required to pay a deposit, service can often be turned on within 24 hours.

Some service providers will allow you to start your service by filling out a form on their Web site. In most cases, however, a Social Security number is required to complete this process electronically. If you do not have a Social Security number, you can still call the company to get your service turned on.

Utilities

If you live in an apartment, some or all of your utilities will probably be included in your rent. For example, you will probably not have to pay for the water supply or for the cost of heating hot water. The cost of heating your apartment is often included in the rent as well. However, if your apartment is heated by electricity, you will most likely have to pay for it. You will have to pay for electricity and, if its used, gas. Renters do not usually have to worry about the costs of garbage removal and other services.

Homeowners, of course, will have to pay for all of the utilities mentioned above: water, electricity, and gas. If your home uses oil or propane, you will need to make arrangements to have fuel delivered to you. Ask your colleagues for recommendations or check the yellow pages of the phone book to find suppliers near you.

Telephone Service

While telephones are not mandatory, virtually all American homes have a telephone. Telephones are a primary method of contact. Telephone service is provided by private companies. Setting up service is much like setting up your utilities: you can contact the telephone company to have the service put in your name or restarted if it was canceled by the previous tenant. And, like the utility company, the telephone company may require a small deposit if you are a new customer with no credit history.

Local Telephone Service

There are several major regional local telephone service providers in the United States. In most cases, their service areas do not overlap, so you will probably not be able to choose from among these. However, recent developments in the telecommunication industry have allowed more competition in both local and long distance telephone service. Some companies, such as AT&T, offer both local and long distance service, although it is not available in all areas.

Service Choices

When you initially set up your local telephone service, you can select from several supplemental services. Each of these carries an extra monthly charge, usually ranging from $2–$12. If you change your mind about a service, you can add or remove it from your account at any time. Many people select one or more of these services to reduce unwanted calls, such as the telemarketing calls that come during dinner, or simply for the added convenience they provide. Please note that, in addition to a monthly fee, some of these services may have a one-time setup fee, so be sure you are fully informed. You may be asked about additional services offered by the phone company, such as insurance against damage to the phone line. A customer service representative at the telephone company will be able to tell you which services are offered and explain their use. A brief description of some of the most popular options follows.

Additional line. If you use a modem or fax machine, you may want to have an additional line. Many families with teenagers—who are notorious for spending hours on the telephone talking to friends—end up having an additional line installed so that Mom and Dad can make an occasional call, too! If your home already has multiple lines installed, they just need to be switched on and added to your account. However, if there is only a single line, another line will have to be installed for an additional fee. The installation can be done by a telephone company technician or an independent contractor—or you can even do it yourself. The telephone company can give you more information on installing additional lines in your home. Additional lines usually incur the same basic fees as your main line.

Call forwarding. Call forwarding allows you to forward your calls to another location. For example, if you are expecting a call, but will be visiting friends, you can enter your friends' phone number into your phone's forwarding system, and all calls that come in to your telephone will be routed to your friend's telephone.

Call waiting. If you are using the telephone when a second call comes in, a special tone alerts you that you have another call. You can switch between the two calls by briefly pressing a designated button (the FLASH button on some phones).

Three-way or conference calling. If you want to talk to two other people at the same time, three-way calling is for you. This feature can be used with both local and long distance calls.

Voice mail. A home voice mail account is an alternative to having an answering machine. And virtually every American household has one or the other! When you are not at home, or even when you are on the telephone, callers can leave you a message. You can access your voice mail account from home or from any other telephone.

Caller Identification (Caller ID). Caller ID allows you to see who is calling you. A small box attached to your telephone line displays and stores incoming calls. You can see who is calling and decide if you want to answer. Although the service is provided by the phone company, you will have to buy the display unit; they are readily available from the phone company or an electronics store.

*69 ("star six nine"). This service allows you to tell you the number of the last person who called you. For example, if you hear the phone ringing when you're fumbling for your keys, but you don't make it to the phone in time, you can dial *69; you will either get a recording that reads the phone number of the person who called you, or it will automatically dial that number back (service varies from area to area). Even if you do not select this option, you can use the feature for a small per-use fee, usually around 75¢.

Unlisted number. If you do not want your telephone number to be printed in the telephone book, you can ask for an unlisted number. It will also mean that your number will not be available to anyone who calls for local directory assistance. An unlisted number can limit the number of marketing calls you receive, since it will not be given out by the telephone company.

Long Distance Service

When you request your local telephone service, you will need to designate a provider for your long distance calls. The three best-known long distance providers are AT&T, MCI, and Sprint. You will then need to contact the long distance provider that you have chosen in order to select a service package. Most companies offer several different packages based on the amount of long distance calls you make, the days and times that you make most of your long distance calls, or the country you are calling; you can choose the one that best meets your needs.

There are also smaller service companies that sometimes have lower fees, but they can be difficult to research. Many specialize in international calls, so the rates can be considerably lower. Ask around for advice on picking a service provider, particularly if you are looking for inexpensive international rates to specific countries.

Selecting your telephone services can seem overwhelming. However, you can change your mind—and your service provider—at any time. Many newcomers find it easiest to start by requesting local service from the major regional provider and selecting one of the major long distance providers. Then you can devote more time to researching the different calling plans available from different providers and deciding if you want to switch providers or service options.

Your Phone Bill

You may get one or two monthly bills. Many service providers are able to combine your local and long distance charges into one bill. In some cases, however, your local and long distance companies may bill you separately. You will probably find that all of the charges on your account are itemized. If your bill just gives the total for long distance charges, you can call the telephone company to request that your bill be itemized. In most locations, there is a base rate that covers all local calls; regional and long distance calls will be listed individually, including the number called, the time of the call, and the charge for the call.

The Telephone Book

Shortly after you set up your local telephone service, you will receive a telephone book. (If you live in a large city, you may receive two books: one for residential and one for business listings.) Your telephone book will have white pages for residential listings and business listings by name, and yellow pages for business listings by category. Most also contain blue pages for federal, state, county, and local government listings; this is usually found between the white and yellow pages.

Your telephone book has a lot of valuable information in it. At the front of the book you will find important numbers (emergency and other), long distance and international dialing instructions, area code lists, and a list of the telephone numbers that you can dial locally. There may also be some maps of your city and information on recreation and entertainment.

Telephone Tips

Here are some practical pieces of information to familiarize yourself with American telephones, both public and private.

- Public phones take coins. The cost of a local call in most places is 50¢; it is lower in some places and higher in others, but the cost will be listed on the telephone. The charge for regional and long distance calls will depend on where you are calling.
- The United States does not have telephone cards that are inserted into the telephones. There are two types of telephone cards, which are used by dialing in the required information; they can be used from any telephone. When you dial using a telephone card, you do not need to insert any coins into the telephone.
  - When you sign up for long distance telephone service for your home phone, you may receive a telephone calling card from the company. This card allows you to make calls when you are away from your home and have the calls charged to your long distance account. There is no charge to get the card, but there is usually a per-call surcharge of about 75¢ when you use the card. Check with your service provider to learn about their policies.
  - You can purchase pre-paid phone cards from many convenience stores, kiosks, drug stores, and discount stores; you can even buy them at the post office. You pay from $5 to about $50 for the card to buy a specified number of minutes. The per-minute cost of the call can vary, so you can

shop around for the best deals. The card is activated when you purchase it. To make a call, follow the dialing instructions printed on the card.

- American telephone numbers consist of a three-digit area code followed by a seven-digit number (the first three digits are called the prefix). Phone numbers are written as follows: (212) 555-1212 or 212-555-1212. If you are dialing within the same area code, dial only the last seven digits (see the next tip for a note on area codes and local calls). If you are calling outside of your area code, you will need to dial a 1, followed by the whole number (i.e., 1-212-555-1212).

- The recent boom of cellular phone use has brought with it the addition of new area codes. Because of this, your city may have multiple area codes assigned to it. Even if the call you are making is local, you will have to dial the area code if it is different from yours.

- There are three codes that designate toll-free calls: 800, 877, and 888. To call a toll-free number, dial the entire 11 digits (don't forget the 1 at the beginning), using the 800, 877, or 888 for the area code. Toll-free calls can be dialed from public telephones without using coins.

- Other special codes to be aware of are 700 and 900. If you dial a 700 or 900 number, you will be charged for the call, usually at rates of $3.95 per minute or more. These numbers are used for profit. For example, you will see television advertisements for psychic hotlines. The advertisement may say that the call is free, but if you read the small print, you will see that only the first minute is free; you are charged by the minute thereafter. "Phone sex" lines are also 700 or 900 numbers. You can ask the telephone company to block calls to 700 and 900 numbers if you would like.

- For all emergency calls, 911 is used almost everywhere in the United States. You can check in your phone book or with your local telephone company to verify that 911 is active in your area. In an emergency, the 911 operator will send the police, fire department, or an ambulance to you. However, this service is available only in English in many places, although areas with large Spanish-speaking communities may also have Spanish-speaking operators.

- You can dial 411 to find a local telephone number. Some telephone companies have recently added long distance information to their 411 service. The charge for this service is set by your local phone company. For example, you may be allowed up to five free local 411 calls per month and 20¢ for additional calls. National 411 listings usually cost 75¢–95¢.
- If national 411 listings are not offered by your telephone company, dial 1 (area code) 555-1212 for directory information in another area code. You will need to know the area code to use this service; you can find a listing of domestic area codes near the front of your telephone book. There is a small fee for this service, usually 50¢–75¢.
- International calls are made by dialing 011, the country code, and the number. You can also call the operator by dialing 0 if you need further assistance in making international calls.
- You can easily find private residence and businesses telephone numbers online as well. Most search engines, such as Yahoo! and Excite, have both white and yellow pages searches. There are also sites specifically for this purpose, such as Anywho.com.
- Most people answer their home phones with a simple "Hello," although some people prefer to identify themselves by saying, for example, "Johnson residence." It's polite to identify yourself when you are calling by saying something like, "Hello, this is Maria. May I speak to John, please?" However, many Americans omit this courtesy and simply ask for the person they are calling. You can ask "Who's calling, please?" if you'd like.

PETS

Americans love their pets. Dogs and cats are the most popular pets, but many people prefer more exotic pets such as birds, fish, or snakes. You will see people walking their dogs at all hours of the day,

but pets are not allowed in most public buildings (Seeing Eye dogs for the blind are the exception; they are allowed everywhere). Apartment buildings may have pet restrictions or even forbid pets. For example, you may be allowed to have a cat or bird, but not a dog. There may also be restrictions on the number of pets you can have in your apartment. If you have a pet, be sure you ask your prospective landlord about pet rules for the building.

Many communities have laws that oblige you to keep your dog on a leash and clean up after it in public places; many require that you obtain a license for your dog. Requirements can vary; your city's Animal Control office can give you the information you need.

If you want to bring your pet with you to the United States, it will need to meet health and customs requirements. Different pets have different requirements; you can obtain specifics for your pet from the United States Department of Agriculture (USDA) at **www.usda.gov**. In general, cats and dogs must be examined at the port of entry for infectious diseases that can be transmitted to humans. Dogs must have been vaccinated for rabies at least 30 days prior to entry (except for puppies less than three months old and dogs coming from places that have been designated by the USDA to be free of rabies). Any animal that appears sick must be examined by a licensed veterinarian.

Veterinary services are very good in the United States. You can locate a veterinarian or animal clinic near you by asking your friends, coworkers, or neighbors for a referral or by looking in the yellow pages of the telephone book.

FINANCIAL MATTERS

Although U.S. dollars are known throughout most of the world, it may be helpful to review the different denominations of currency you will see during your stay. Paper notes come in denominations of $100, $50, $20, $10, $5, $2 (these are only printed occasionally), and $1. The U.S. Treasury is implementing a new design to make counterfeiting more difficult. There are newly designed bills in circulation for all but the $1 and $2 bills. Both the old and the new bills can be used interchangeably. Although $100 and $50 bills are not uncommon, it can sometimes be difficult to spend them, especially in smaller shops where you often see signs saying that the establishment will not accept bills larger than $20. Larger bills can be exchanged for smaller denominations at any bank.

American coins come in different sizes and colors. Currently in circulation are $1, 50¢ (rarely seen), 25¢ (quarter), 10¢ (dime), 5¢ (nickel), and 1¢ (penny) coins. You may see several different types of $1 coins: silver dollars (now rarely seen in circulation; most are in the hands of collectors), Susan B. Anthony coins (which bear her portrait in honor of her work as a suffragette; these are easily confused with quarters and are unpopular), and the newer gold-colored dollar fea-

turing Sacagawea, the Native American (Shoshone) woman who guided Lewis and Clark on their exploratory expedition through the American West.

You may also find other unusual coins in your change. For example, the U.S. Mint is currently issuing a series of state quarters. There are 50 designs in total, one for each state. The design on the reverse of the quarter celebrates a state by depicting a historical scene, building, or other unique feature. A new state design will be issued every 10 weeks until 2008. Older coins that are occasionally found are buffalo nickels (nickels with the profile of a Native American man on the front and a buffalo on the back were minted between 1913 and 1938) and wheaties (pennies with two springs of wheat on the back). These older coins can be used, but some have more value as collectors' items.

Personal Banking

One of your first tasks when you move to the United States will be to open a checking account. You will need checks to pay your bills and an account where you can deposit your paychecks. Checking accounts are easy to open, but it may take you some time to wade through the available choices. First, you will have to first choose a bank. Then you will have to choose which type of checking account meets your needs. To find out what services are offered by a particular bank, you can visit them in person, call them, or visit their Web site. If you are unsure what type of account is best for you, it can be helpful to visit the bank in person and speak to a new-accounts representative. If you do, you do not have to make an immediate decision; you can simply gather information from several institutions to take home to compare.

There are many different types of financial institutions to choose from, such as commercial banks, trust companies, and savings banks. Historically, each type of banking institution played a very specific role, but changes in the past couple of decades have blurred the distinctions between these institutions. Today, they all provide similar services.

When you are selecting a bank, you will want to be sure that the institution is insured by the FDIC (Federal Deposit Insurance Corporation); most U.S. banks are. When you deposit your money in an FDIC-insured institution, your money is insured for up to $100,000. This means that if the bank fails, your money, up to this amount, is safe. Therefore, if your cash assets total more than $100,000, you will want to explore ways to maintain full coverage. Note that FDIC insurance is per category account. Keeping two accounts in one bank does not automatically increase your coverage; the accounts must be in different ownership categories. For example, let's say your total deposits are $175,000. If you and your spouse have two accounts in the same bank, both with joint ownership, only $100,000 is insured. However, if you have one account in your name and one account in joint ownership with your spouse, the full amount would be insured. Of course, if you and your spouse open two joint accounts at separate banks, you will be fully covered. For more information on protecting your money, speak with a financial advisor or visit **www.fdic.gov**.

Credit unions can offer an alternative way to do your banking. However, you must be eligible for membership in the credit union to open accounts there. Credit unions are nonprofit financial institutions that serve a group of people with a common bond. Some large companies and many federal and municipal agencies have credit unions for their employees. People in certain occupations and trades, such as teaching, have access to credit unions because of this affiliation, and there are even credit unions open to residents of some communities. As a credit union member, you are also an owner and have voting privileges on issues that affect the union. Credit unions offer similar services to those available in banks: checking and savings accounts, loans, and investment services. If you are eligible to join a credit union, you will want to be sure that it is insured by the NCUA (National Credit Union Administration), an independent governmental agency that charters and insures credit unions, to be certain that your deposits are safe. You can find more information about the NCUA at **www.ncua.gov**.

Types of Accounts

When you are ready to open your account, you may be able to apply for an account online or over the telephone. However, many banks offer these options to resident aliens who already have a Social Security number. You will need to bring a piece of identification with your picture on it, such as your passport, and proof of your address. This can be a copy of your lease or a telephone or utility bill. Most accounts require an initial deposit, but the amount will vary depending on the type of account. For a basic account, the initial deposit may be as little as $20.

Most banks offer an entire menu of checking accounts and have a corresponding range of fees. A basic account (the name of the account will vary by institution) often allows you to write a limited number of checks per month and make ATM (Automatic Teller Machine) transactions for a small monthly fee. If you go over the specified amount of transactions, you are charged an additional fee. Other accounts offer more flexibility but also incur a larger monthly fee; however, this fee may be waived if you keep a certain amount of money in the account. You can also opt to open an interest-bearing account, but the amount of checks you can write on that account is usually restricted.

Many people find that what works best for them is a combination of accounts. Many banks encourage you to keep all of your deposits with them by waiving fees if the total of all your accounts is above a certain point.

In addition to being able to write checks on your account, most banks offer supplemental services. Some examples are:

ATM or debit cards. ATM or debit cards are a normal part of the average American's life. You will probably be issued an ATM or debit card with any checking account you open. They give you easy access to your money around the clock and help the bank cut down on overhead costs as well. An ATM card allows you to deposit or withdraw money from your account at a machine. Most banks, however, now use debit cards. Like ATM cards, debit cards allow you to access your account at machines. However, unlike ATM cards, debit cards can also be used in stores. When you make your purchase, you swipe your debit card, then enter your PIN (personal identification number). Debit cards offer the benefits of checks without having to actually write the check. The money is directly deducted from your account, just as is done with a check. Both ATM and debit cards can be used virtually anywhere. However, most banks charge a fee ($1–$2.50) when you use your card in another bank's machine. In addition, some machines, especially those located in convenience stores and other non-bank locations, charge another transaction fee.

Overdraft protection. Have you ever written a check, then realized that you don't have enough money in the bank to cover it? Most banks offer overdraft protection. Simply put, if you write a check but don't have enough money in your account, the bank will pay the check anyway. Of course, this service is rarely free, so be sure to inquire about any accompanying fees.

Direct deposit. Very often, you can arrange to have your paycheck deposited directly into your bank account. This is done through your employer, not your bank. Your payroll department should be able to provide you with information and application forms. Having your paycheck deposited directly saves you a trip to the bank, and the money will be available to you immediately.

Automatic payments. If you make regular payments, you can have them automatically deducted from your account. For example, if you are making a monthly car payment, you can authorize your bank to make the payment for you. This can help ensure that your payments are on time and can cut down on the amount of time you spend paying bills.

Online banking. Most banks now offer you the ability to do some or all of your banking online. Checking your account balance and account activity is generally free. More and more banks are making this information available for download to your financial software, such as Quicken or Microsoft Money. You may have to pay an additional monthly fee if you would like to perform transactions via the Internet. This service allows you to pay your bills online. You can even write checks in advance—to be paid on the date you specify—or have the money automatically deducted from your account on a monthly basis.

Paying the Bills

You will get many monthly bills, such as your utility, telephone, and credit card bills. Although you can go in person to the utility or telephone company to pay your bill with cash, most people pay their bills by sending a check in the mail. Never send cash in the mail. Your bill will have a pay stub that you should detach and return with your check.

If you have to pay a bill or two before you get a checking account set up, you can get a money order at the post office and at most banks. You can pay for the money order with cash or a credit card; a small fee is charged for each money order you buy.

If you find yourself close to the payment deadline for a particular bill, some companies, such as credit card companies, can accept your payment over the telephone. In this situation, you will need to provide information about your bank and your checking account; the money can then be deducted directly from your account. Note, though, that it can take a day or two for the payment to be processed, so it's best not to wait until the due date to pay a bill.

Recently, many companies have made it possible for customers to pay their bills online; you will have to contact the company to find out if they offer this service. Even if that company does not, more and more banks have online bill payment options, and even the United States Post Office has a service that allows you to both receive and pay your bills electronically.

Cash or Credit?

The United States is no longer a cash-based society. People use credit or debit cards to pay for everything from a restaurant meal to their groceries to gasoline. Credit cards are accepted almost everywhere, and more and more establishments can accept debit cards as well. (Some notable exceptions are in small restaurants, which may only take cash; if you are short on cash, be sure you ask if you can pay with a credit card before you sit down.) The most commonly used credit cards are MasterCard, Visa, American Express, Discover, and Diners Club. Most stores and restaurants have a sign on the door or by the cash register that will tell you which credit cards you can use there.

SOCIALIZING

Meeting People and Making Friends

Americans are friendly, and it is usually quite easy to meet people. The best advice for meeting new friends is to do something you enjoy. Join a tennis club or a yoga class, become a member of a stamp club or a reading circle, go to a lecture on art history, or volunteer at an animal shelter. Even taking your dog for a walk in the park or your child to the playground in your neighborhood park can be an opportunity to meet new people.

You don't have to go out of your way to meet people in the United States. People meet in many ways, often doing the things they do on a daily basis. For example, if you like to work out, you can strike up a conversation with someone in your aerobics class at the gym. Many people find that their children provide a multitude of ways to meet other parents. If you have children, join the school PTA (Parent-

Teacher Association), coach your child's soccer team, or be a Boy Scout or Girl Scout troop leader. Churches, temples, synagogues, and other houses of worship also offer opportunities to socialize with other people. Many of them have potluck dinners where everyone contributes something: a casserole, a dessert, a salad, or another dish. Check the newsletter for other social gatherings or group meetings, such as those for singles and young couples, as well as activities such as a church basketball league, field trips, and so on.

You can also find ways to combine professional networking and socializing. Many professions have a national association with local chapters throughout the country. Even if you moved with your spouse or partner and are not able to work in the United States, these organizations can keep you in touch with your profession and allow you to meet people who share your interests.

There are many other national or local organizations that can offer both working and non-working partners the opportunity to network and develop skills as well as to make friends and have fun. Some examples are Toastmasters, an organization that helps its members perfect their public speaking skills, and Rotary, Lions Club, or Kiwanis Club, all of which are organizations that combine socializing with service to the community.

If you have a hobby, chances are good that others share your passion, so you may find a formal or informal club of your fellow philatelists, hikers, or bird watchers. The library can be a good starting place when you are looking for a local organization to join, especially in towns and smaller cities. Many libraries have a community bulletin board where local meetings are posted.

Volunteering is another good way to meet people. Around 50% of Americans volunteer an average of about four hours a week. If you would like to donate your time to a worthy cause, it's easy to find one. If there is a cause you are particularly interested in, you can simply call the appropriate organization. For example, if you like animals, call your local animal shelter; if you want to teach people to read, call the library. Most of these places are easily found in your telephone book. If you want to see what kind of volunteering opportunities there are in your community, you can look in your local newspaper—

many carry weekly information on the activities of service organizations. You can also contact the United Way (**www.unitedway.org**), which can help you find an organization that is in need of what you have to offer.

You might also find friendships among your neighbors. Of course, some neighbors are friendlier than others. Like most places, big cities tend to encourage anonymity while people in small towns tend to know one another more. However, neighbors in towns and cities alike are quite willing to bemoan the lack of rain or tell you about their child's or grandchild's latest accomplishment. Some communities and neighborhoods actively encourage people to get to know one another. If you live in an apartment complex, there may be occasional gatherings, allowing residents to meet one another and socialize. If you live in a suburban neighborhood, several neighbors might get together for a barbeque in someone's backyard; there may even be a party for the entire street, where each family brings some food to share and everyone grills hamburgers, plays games, and generally has fun.

People also socialize with their coworkers. This is especially true for single people, who often go out after work for a drink or dinner. If a closer friendship develops, you may find yourself getting together on weekends as well. You might meet another couple for dinner and a movie or meet a coworker to see a basketball game. Some companies host one or more annual gatherings for their employees and their families. This may be the company Christmas party or a summer "family day." These are occasions to get together with your coworkers and their families outside of working hours and just have fun.

As you begin to meet new people, you should know that many newcomers to the United States find Americans to be very open and friendly. However, terminology can be misleading. The word "friend" is loosely used in the United States. Although there is certainly an English word to use for people you do not know very well— "acquaintance"—that word is not often used by Americans. You won't hear someone say, "I'd like you to meet my acquaintance, Larry." Even if he just met Larry ten minutes ago, he will say, "I'd like you to meet my friend, Larry." In fact, most Americans have a wide circle of "friends" who are really acquaintances and only a handful of true friends.

Friendships in the United States are also often temporary. Americans tend to move a lot, from city to city as well as from job to job. And with each move, many friendships—or acquaintanceships—fall by the wayside. You will probably find that most Americans you meet live far away from where they grew up and that few of them are still in regular contact with childhood friends. Don't let this dissuade you from making new American friends; just approach it knowing the rules by which Americans play. After all, you can have fun with people who share a common bond, even if that bond is not as strong as the ones to which you are accustomed. In fact, you will no doubt discover that most Americans are very open to adding new friends to their social circle and will welcome you to into the fold.

Be My Guest: Being on Your Best Behavior as a Host or Guest

Americans often entertain at home. Of course, you will want to dress appropriately, but these gatherings are seldom formal. For example, if you are invited to a summer barbeque, shorts or jeans are probably acceptable. Jeans or slacks are appropriate for a casual dinner or party with friends. Some occasions do require something a little more formal. For dressier occasions, you will see men wearing slacks with a jacket (often without a tie) and women wearing a variety of styles, including slacks, pant suits, or skirts. Feel free to wear what you would wear in your own country for a similar occasion. If you are unsure, you can ask the host for advice.

You should be more or less on time for most occasions, especially if a meal is being served. If you arrive more than a few minutes early, you will probably catch your hosts finishing up the last-minute preparations; you have room to arrive 5–10 minutes late, but no later than that. If you are going to a larger party, especially an informal one, you have a lot more leeway in when you can arrive. At these types of gatherings, some of the attendees invariably arrive 30 minutes to an hour after it starts.

Most dinners or parties do not have a specified end time. At larger parties, you will see when others begin to leave and can time your exit accordingly. At a smaller party you will have to rely on your own judgment to be sure you do not overstay your welcome, since your hosts are unlikely to tell you when it is time to leave. During the week, small parties usually end between 10:00 and 11:00 PM; on the weekend, they can last longer (12:00 AM), depending on the type of party and people attending.

If you are invited to an informal dinner, you can offer to help your hosts set up by setting the table, pouring drinks, etc. Then, when dinner is over, your hosts may clear the table, but they will usually postpone washing the dishes until their guests leave. You can offer to help with whatever cleaning they are doing. At more formal occasions, which are often catered, you are not expect to offer to help.

Bringing a gift when you are invited to someone's home for dinner, a party, or other special occasion is the courteous thing to do. When you receive the invitation, you can ask if you can bring something. Your host may reply that it would be nice if you could bring a bottle of wine or something similar, or he or she may tell you not to bring anything. If it's an informal dinner, you may even want to offer to bring some food; in fact, your American friends would probably enjoy trying a dish from your home country. Even when the host declines the offer, most people still like to bring a little something. Typical gifts for the hosts are wine or a bouquet of flowers. For a more elaborate occasion, a bottle of scotch or brandy (if you know what your host drinks) or a floral arrangement are appropriate.

The gift should be presented when you arrive, and it will probably be opened immediately. Flowers are presented with the wrapper still on them. Wine or liquor may be consumed at dinner or afterward, unless your host has already chosen something special to serve with the meal.

If you would like to take flowers to your host, you do not have to worry a great deal about any hidden significances. Few flowers are associated with anything in particular to Americans. Roses are the exception. Roses, especially red ones, are usually given romantically. Nevertheless, all flowers are acceptable if they are part of a mixed bouquet.

If you are invited to someone's home for a longer stay, such as a weekend at a friend's vacation home, you should give your hosts a nice gift to show your appreciation. You can bring something along with you to give to them at the end of your stay, or send it to them afterward. Another alternative is to take your hosts out to dinner as a way of thanking them.

Don't be surprised if friends ask for a tour of your home or if your hosts offer to show you theirs. And even though Americans are fond of saying "Oh, just drop by any time," they usually don't mean it. If you would like to visit a friend, call first to schedule a visit.

Dating

If you are a single person moving to the United States, or if you have teenagers, you probably have some questions about dating. Although it is certainly acceptable for a woman to ask a man on a date, it is more often the man who approaches the woman.

For both adults and teens, holding hands and walking arm-in-arm in public are perfectly acceptable. In recent years, it has become common to see more overt or lewd displays, such as extended kissing or fondling, in public areas like movie theaters and malls.

Relationships can blossom just about anywhere. People meet at work, in clubs and bars, at church, through personal ads placed in the newspaper, or on the Internet. Common sense should always be used when agreeing to a date with someone you just met, such as meeting in a restaurant or other public place.

First dates usually take place in a nice restaurant or cafe, not in the local dive. Subsequent dates could be any number of things from a movie to dancing to a picnic. In the initial stages of a romantic relationship, it is usually the man who pays for dinner and entertainment, although a woman is free to pay if she wishes. Even if the man issues the invitation, a woman may wish to split the bill or pay for the movie if the man buys the dinner, for example. Depending on the financial status of the individuals, both may contribute in later stages of the relationship.

Adolescents and teens tend to congregate and socialize in

groups. The age at which children begin to date and have boyfriends or girlfriends varies. Many parents agree that their kids should wait until they are at least in high school to begin dating. However, some allow their children to date several years earlier.

Though Americans exercise a certain amount of openness when it comes to dating and premarital sex, many attitudes toward sex remain fairly conservative. Sex has a mystery and near-taboo about it that it has become very powerful; it is probably the number one tool for selling consumer goods in the United States. American movies, television shows, and publications are full of violent scenes, while sex is much more censored. As a result, children are generally shielded from nudity, and sexuality becomes something forbidden, something to be hidden. In this respect, American adolescents and teens can be less mature about sex than some of their international counterparts. It can be quite an adjustment for newcomers, who may be more comfortable with their bodies.

This is not to say that American teens do not have sexual intercourse; indeed, many people are very concerned about statistics that say many children, boys and girls alike, have sexual experiences at a very early age, even in the preteen years. However, because the current values make sex something that must be hidden, children often begin having sexual encounters without being taught about the risks of sexually transmitted diseases and pregnancy.

SEXUAL ORIENTATION

People who are gay, bisexual, or transgendered find that larger cities offer a more open and friendly environment. In most smaller towns it is not as acceptable to be open about such things. Many large cities have a gay neighborhood, such as Greenwich Village in New York City.

Being openly gay, bisexual, or transgendered in the sphere of your personal life is an individual choice. Being open in the workplace, however, is more complex. In matters of sexual orientation, most of America, especially corporate America, has an implicit attitude of "don't ask, don't tell." That is to say, although there are laws that protect people from discrimination as a result of their sexual orientation, it can be very difficult to be openly gay, bisexual, or transgendered in the workplace. The degree of acceptance of less popular sexual orientations varies from industry to industry, from company to company, and of course, from person to person.

There is much controversy surrounding the issue of sexual orientation in the United States. While recent strides have been made in some areas, other events have had the opposite effect. One of the central issues is that of the rights of same-sex partners. Vermont is as of yet the only state that has officially legalized same-sex marriages, and same-sex partners throughout the rest of the United States do not have the same rights that a married couple—even a common-law marriage—have, including parental rights, health insurance coverage, and tax benefits. However, more and more companies, universities, and city governments are beginning to offer domestic partnership benefits such as health insurance to same-sex partners.

ETIQUETTE

Greetings and Conversations

The typical American greeting is a smile, often accompanied by a nod, wave, or a verbal greeting, such as "Hi." Handshakes are also common, and are appropriate for both men and women; some men wait for a woman to extend her hand first. Handshakes are firm, but quick; light handshakes can be regarded as a sign of weakness or indifference. Embraces and kisses are generally reserved for family and close friends. It is not common to see men embracing, and when you do, there is generally a handshake maintaining some distance between them.

Although Americans generally keep an arm's length of distance between themselves when they converse, there may be some casual touching, including back slapping or arm punching.

Americans will very quickly invite you to use their first names, and will use yours. Generally speaking, if someone uses your first name, you have implicit permission to use theirs, although it is more courteous to address people who are much older than you by "Mr." or "Mrs." and the last name. Nicknames are common, and some people may shorten your name. The title of "Dr." may be used for medical doctors and dentists, or persons who hold a PhD. College professors are addressed as Professor and judges are addressed as Judge or Your Honor. These titles are used with the person's last name, such as Dr. Peterson or Professor Kelly. Titles are used in the law enforcement field (Officer Richards, Detective Burke) and in politics (Senator Wilson, Mayor Jones); these titles can also be used without the person's name. Most other professional titles, such as attorney or engineer, are not used.

Children might address adults with Mr. or Ms. and the person's first or last name. For example, a teacher might be Mr. Waters and someone who works in the daycare center may be Ms. Mary. Close family friends may be called Aunt or Uncle as a compromise be-tween the informality of using the first name and the formality of Mr. or Mrs. However, some children, especially teenagers, may be accus-tomed to addressing their parents' friends by their first names.

"How are you?" is a common greeting, but it is not an inquiry after your health or general state of being. An appropriate response is "Fine, thank you" or even something more casual such as "Not too bad" or "Hanging in there." You can follow your response with "How are you?" If someone asks you how you are as they pass you in the hall, they are not expecting to hear about your backache or about the fight you had with your landlord.

A common conversation starter with someone you don't know is "So, what do you do?" referring to your occupation. General topics of discussion with new acquaintances include jobs, sports, television, movies, books, etc. Don't be surprised to encounter conversations about dieting and exercise. International visitors and expatriates often find that the Americans they meet are curious about them and their home countries, especially if they have not met many people from abroad. Americans often begin conversations with a compli-ment. They compliment each other as a way of being friendly and showing an interest in someone. Newcomers often get the impres-sion that they have the world's best wardrobe, because virtually everything they wear receives a compliment!

It is best to wait for personal information, such as marital status or whom a person may be dating, to be offered. Be prepared for ques-tions about the occupation of your spouse or partner. Wait until you know someone well to introduce topics such as religion or politics. Even then, recognize that many Americans prefer to avoid argu-ments and are reluctant to get involved in a debate on controversial issues with friends.

Other Important Items

While courtesy and politeness are appreciated, women should not expect that men will hold doors for them or stand up when they enter the room.

Lines (queues) are sacred. Whether you are standing "on line" (in the Northeast) or "in line" in the rest of the United States, do not break rank! The other people in line will glare at you, and there will probably be some muttering; someone may even say something to you.

Smoking is becoming more and more uncommon in the United States and is forbidden in many restaurants and public places. If you are in a public place and would like to smoke, first ask those around you if they object. In someone's home, be sure you ask your host if it's okay to smoke. Many nonsmokers—and even some smokers— like to keep their homes free of smoke and would prefer that you step outside for a cigarette.

GIFT-GIVING

Gift-giving in the United States is most often associated with a holiday or another celebration and is usually reserved for family and very close friends. Here are the occasions when gifts may be given.

Christmas. Christmas is the time of year when the most gifts are given. However, the gift-giving is usually within the family, although some people exchange gifts with close friends. Many American parents shower their children with Christmas gifts.

Valentine's Day. February 14 is Valentine's Day, a day for public and private affection. On this day, most married and dating couples exchange cards and gifts, such as chocolates in special heart-shaped boxes or jewelry. School age children often exchange valentines, special cards with a Valentine's Day theme. Your child's teacher can tell you what is customary in that school.

Birthdays. If you have children, they may be invited to their friends' birthday parties, or you may want to have a birthday party for your child. Adults generally do not have birthday parties, although some people like to throw a bash for milestone birthdays, such as the 30th or 50th. As a general rule, if you are invited to a party, you should bring a gift. If your child is invited to a party, you can call the parents of the birthday honoree to ask what the child would like to receive. At children's birthday parties, it is also customary for the guests to receive party favors, usually small gifts such as candy, pencils, stickers, etc. If you would like to acknowledge the birthday of a friend or coworker, it is fine to give him or her a card. You could also invite him or her for a drink or a meal (often with other coworkers), if you have a particularly close work relationship.

Life's milestones. Weddings, births, and significant anniversaries are cause for celebration. Prior to a wedding, a bride will have a bridal shower, hosted by her maid of honor, and the groom will have a bachelor party, hosted by his best man. Customarily, only women attend a bridal shower and only men attend a bachelor party. Similarly, an expectant mother will usually have a baby shower, thrown for her by her friends. When a couple reaches a milestone wedding anniversary, such as the 25th or 50th, their family and friends may host a party in their honor. If you attend any of these events, you should bring a gift. You can ask friends for help in selecting a gift or contact the host of the event to get suggestions. In addition, most people who receive an invitation to a wedding send a gift even if they are not able to attend.

Family holidays. Other occasions when people exchange cards and gifts are Mother's Day and Father's Day. However, gifts are given only to family members.

At work. In general, personal gifts to coworkers are not often given. (See the section on "Business Gifts" in the "Business Step-by-Step" chapter for more information on business gifts.) If you work closely with a group of people, you may be asked to contribute a few dollars to buy a group gift for a coworker who is retiring, getting married, or having a baby. In some offices, birthdays are celebrated, but usually only with a cake and a card signed by everyone in the office. At Christmas, your office may have a "Secret Santa" gift exchange. Participation is not mandatory. If you choose to participate, you will be given the name of a coworker for whom you will buy a gift; there is usually a limit to the amount of money that should be spent on the gift. The gift is given anonymously, often at an office Christmas party. In some offices, especially if you work with a small group of people, you may receive a small Christmas gift from your coworkers. Take your gift-giving cues from your coworkers.

FOOD

In Restaurants

If you are invited to a restaurant by friends, be prepared to pay for your share. At the end of the meal, you can ask how much your share is, or your host may say that he will get the check. If your host does pay for the dinner, you should reciprocate so that the balance between hosting remains roughly equal.

If you go out for drinks with friends, each person will probably be responsible for buying his or her own drinks. In some cases, people will take turn buying rounds until the cost is relatively evenly distributed. Of course, this means that you will be drinking the same number of drinks as there are people, so don't start the process unless you are prepared to have the required number of drinks.

If you are a woman, single or married, it is acceptable for you to go to a restaurant or bar alone or with a man who is not your spouse. Women who are by themselves or with other women may be approached by men in bars; it is up to the woman whether or not she wants to engage in a conversation.

In many moderate- to low-priced restaurants, your waiter or waitress ("server") will introduce himself or herself to you with, "Hi, I'm Chris and I'll be serving you this evening." You can summon the waiter by raising your hand to get his attention, or even call out to him as he passes your table. If your waiter is not in sight, you can ask another waiter to summon your waiter. In better restaurants, use only a raised hand to summon the waiter or catch his eye and make a small motion with your head.

Most of the time, dinners in restaurants are quite informal. Although you should wait until everyone at the table has been served to

begin eating, if your dinner is delayed, you can urge the others to start so their food does not get cold. Soups and salads are served before the meal. You may eat your soup or salad when it arrives if others at the table did not order one.

Americans enjoy sharing food. Friends often split an appetizer and ask if you want to take a bite or two from their plate to try what they ordered.

After you have eaten, the waiter or waitress will bring your bill. You will most often pay the waiter or waitress. However, in some less formal restaurants, such as diners, you will need to take your bill to the cash register to pay. Ask your waiter or waitress if you are not sure where to pay. You can leave the cash tip on the table, or you can add it to the total if you are paying by credit card. See the section on tipping at the end of this chapter.

Knives are used only for cutting and spreading. Americans will cut several pieces of meat with the knife in their right hand, then switch the knife and fork, eating with their right hand. If you are accustomed to keeping your knife in your right hand, that is fine, although you should be careful that you don't bump your neighbor's elbows. Although not considered good manners, you will notice that many Americans eat with their hands, and sometimes their elbows, on the table.

At the end of the meal, you can ask that the remaining food be wrapped up for you to take home; this is commonly called a "doggie bag." Note that this is in restaurants only, not when you are at someone's home.

Toasts are infrequent and informal. If you are celebrating something in particular, a brief toast such as, "Here's to you—happy birthday!" is fine; this may or may not be accompanied by a clinking of glasses. At a more formal occasion, such as a wedding reception or rehearsal dinner (a dinner that takes place the night before the wedding), a longer, more formal toast or speech might be given. However, when you are out with friends for no particular reason, the most you are likely to do is raise your glass slightly and say, "Cheers!"

HEALTH AND SAFETY

Health

The United States offers a wide variety of high-quality health care in every area from dentistry to surgery. It's a good idea to find a doctor you like before you need one. You can ask coworkers, friends, and neighbors for recommendations. Most people have a family doctor, also called a general practitioner or internist, who does general checkups and who is the first doctor they visit when they are sick or injured. The family doctor can then make referrals to appropriate specialists, such as surgeons or orthopedic doctors. If you have children, their primary doctor may be a pediatrician. A woman may also make regular visits to a gynecologist or an obstetrician (if she is pregnant) without a referral from her primary doctor. Doctors and dentists alike encourage preventative health care with annual or biannual checkups.

You should be prepared to wait when you visit a doctor or dentist. You are expected to be on time for your appointment, but the doctor is not. Between the overbooking that is common in doctor's offices and patients who get squeezed in for immediate care, wait times are often long. However, they should not be unreasonable; if you have a lengthy wait every time you go to a particular doctor's office, perhaps it's time to consider finding a new doctor. It is extremely rare for doctors to come to you; house calls are unheard of in most places.

Emergency or after-hours care is available at the hospital. Some clinics also have extended hours and are able to treat minor emergencies. You are expected to pay for treatment when you arrive, or at least prove that you can pay. This may mean showing your insurance card or giving them a credit card that can be used to pay for treatment. However, in a true emergency, a hospital will not refuse you treatment.

Insurance

Health insurance is not mandatory, but it is a good idea to have it. The cost of health care in the United States can be very expensive; a simple office visit can cost more than $100. Most companies offer health insurance benefits to their employees. Because they are insuring a large group of people, the cost to the individual is fairly low. Many companies pay for a portion of their employees' insurance costs; the remainder is deducted from the employees' paychecks on a regular schedule.

Your company may offer several types of insurance, so you will have to determine which is the best for you. Most companies offer at least basic health insurance coverage; some also have supplemental dental and eye care insurance as well. You will need to select the type of insurance you want and fill out the necessary forms before you are covered. Insurance is usually handled through your company's human resources or benefits department. Contact that department if you have any questions about the policies offered or if you need help deciphering the information.

If you will be traveling out of the country, be sure to check to see if you will be covered under the insurance you choose; you may need additional insurance for international travel. Often the procedure for getting medical attention while you are away from home is complicated, even if you are traveling within the United States. You may be required to get approval from your insurance company before seeking treatment for anything but the most dire of emergencies, so be sure you understand the policies and procedures of your insurance provider.

When you visit a doctor, clinic, or hospital, you will need to show your insurance card; you may also be required to show a piece of identification with your picture on it, such as your driver's license or passport.

Following are some common insurance structures:

HMO. A Health Maintenance Organization (HMO) is a group of doctors who join together in an effort to manage health-care costs. Many HMOs have their own facilities with doctors on staff; other HMOs are a network of independent physicians. Whatever the structure of the HMO, you must select all of your doctors from the HMO's network in order for your medical costs to be covered. If you need the services of a specialist, you will first have to visit your primary care physician for a referral to a doctor who is part of the HMO's network. When you visit the doctor, you will make a co-payment, and the insurance covers any additional expenses. The amount of the co-payment depends on your particular policy, but they are usually between $5 and $20 per visit. Prescribed medications also require a similar co-payment.

PPO. A Preferred Provider Organization (PPO) is a network of independent physicians, but it usually offers more flexibility than an HMO because you do not need to get a referral to specialists. However, if you elect to go to a doctor who is not a member of the PPO, you will have to pay for some or all of the cost of treatment. Like HMOs, most PPOs require a co-payment for each doctor's visit or prescription filled.

Fee-for-service. This is the most flexible type of insurance plan but also the most costly. A fee-for-service plan allows you to use any physician you desire, but you may incur more expenses. You will pay for medical treatment up to a predetermined point; this is called your deductible. The insurance will then pay a predetermined fee for any treatment thereafter. This fee may not be enough to cover the amount charged by the physician; in this case, you are responsible for any remaining costs. For example, if you have a $250 deductible, you will pay for your medical treatment until you have spent $250 in one year. Once you have reached the $250 limit, your insurance will pay for further treatment. However, if your doctor charges you $120 for an exam and the insurance guidelines say that the fee for that service is $100, you pay the additional $20 out-of-pocket.

Prescriptions and Other Medicines

When your doctor gives you a prescription, you will need to take it to a pharmacy to get it filled. There are no apothecaries in the United States; pharmacies have been incorporated into other types of stores. You will find pharmacies in drug stores, supermarkets, and even in discount stores. Pharmacists are all licensed and are very knowledgeable, so you should feel free to talk with the pharmacist about any questions or concerns you have. It's always a good idea to let both your doctor and your pharmacist know if you are taking other medication before you begin taking a new medicine, since many medications should not be used in combination. If your prescription calls for a refill when you have emptied the bottle, you can simply call the pharmacy to let them know that you will be coming in to pick up your refill. They should have it ready when you arrive or will give you a time when you can pick it up.

If your insurance card covers prescriptions, you will need to go to a pharmacy that accepts your type of insurance. Most pharmacies have a sign listing the insurance plans that they can accept, or you can call to ask. When you pick up your prescription, you will have to show your insurance card and make a co-payment if one is required by your insurance plan. You may also be required to show some identification in order to pick up your prescription.

Many medications do not require a prescription. For example, allergy, flu, or cold medication can be purchased without a prescription. These are called over-the-counter drugs. Of course, over-the-counter drugs are not as potent as those prescribed by a doctor, so if you have a serious problem, your doctor can probably prescribe something more powerful. If you have any questions about the use of over-the-counter medication, you can ask the pharmacist for assistance.

POST OFFICE

The United States Post Office is a federal governmental agency. Mail service in the U.S. is generally safe, efficient, and reliable. A letter sent from coast to coast will generally arrive in three to four days. Most mail, such as bills, correspondence, etc., is sent first-class. First-class postcards cost slightly less than first-class mail. Some nonstandard size envelopes may cost a little more. Postal rates are subject to change; be sure to confirm the current rates by calling your local post office or visiting the U.S. Post Office's Web site at **www.usps.gov**.

In addition to standard first-class mail service, the post office offers many other mailing and shipping options. Following are some of the more popular services used. Most of these services can be combined to meet your needs in any particular circumstance. If you are unsure what service you need, a postal employee at your local post office can give you some suggestions. Some of the services require you to fill out a form; these can be obtained from the post office, and some are even available on the post office's Web site.

Priority mail. Delivery to most domestic locations is within two days. The cost is based on the weight of the piece mailed; for packages over five pounds, the cost is based on both the weight of the package and the distance it's being sent. There are some size and weight restrictions. If you prefer, the post office will pick up your parcel from your home or office for an additional fee; you can call your local post office to schedule a pick up.

Express mail. The post office can deliver your letter or package by noon the next day, including weekends and holidays. Cost is based on the weight of the piece and the distance it is being sent.

Insured mail. If you are shipping something valuable, you may want to insure it against loss or damage. Coverage up to $5,000 is available for first-class and priority mail; the fee will depend on the value of the contents.

Certificate of mailing. If you need proof that you mailed something, such as your tax returns, a certificate of mailing is available. Note that the certificate of mailing does not provide proof of delivery, only of mailing. This service is available for first-class and priority mail as well as for some other classes of service.

Certified mail. This service provides you with a mailing receipt; the post office tracks the item and keeps a record of delivery information. This is available for first-class and priority mail.

Delivery confirmation. If you want to receive information about the date and time of delivery of the item, delivery confirmation is available for priority and other mail services for a small fee.

International Mail and Shipping

There are five main categories of international mail: Global Express Guaranteed (GXG), Global Express Mail (EMS), Global Priority Mail (GPM), Airmail, and Economy. A brief explanation of each follows, but more information about rates and services to specific countries can be obtained from the U.S. Post Office Web site or your local post office. Additional commercial services are available for business mailings.

Global Express Guaranteed (GXG). GXG provides expedited delivery to more than 200 countries for packages up to 70 pounds. The cost of shipping depends on the weight of the package and the destination country. The speed of service also depends on the destination country; the post office will give you the deliver-by date and guarantees delivery within that time frame or the shipping cost will be refunded. GXG is a service provided in conjunction with DHL Worldwide Express, an international expediting service. Items are insured up to $100; you can purchase additional insurance.

Global Express Mail (EMS). Express mail service is available to more than 175 countries. Cost and speed of delivery depend on the size of the item and the destination country. Because this service works in conjunction with the destination country's own mail infrastructure, there is no money-back guarantee. Items are insured up to $500, but you can purchase additional insurance. Return receipt service is available at no additional charge from some countries.

Global Priority Mail (GPM). This airmail service provides reliable service to many countries around the world. Items sent by global priority mail receive priority handling both in the United States and in the destination country. Packages up to 4 lbs and the cost of shipping depends on the weight of the item and the destination country.

Airmail and economy. Letters, postcards, and packages can be sent by airmail or economy mail. The cost and speed of delivery depend on the weight of the item and the destination country. Airmail delivery is faster than economy, but will cost more.

Sending and Receiving Mail

Mail in most places in the United States is delivered Monday through Saturday. No mail is delivered on Sundays or on federal holidays. (However, you can have letters and packages delivered on Sundays and holidays by using special services such as express mail.) If a package or an item requiring a signature arrives when you are not home, the postal carrier will leave a note on your door with instructions on how to retrieve your mail. You may be able to sign the note, authorizing the mail carrier to leave the package next to your front door, or you may be instructed to go to your local post office to pick up the item.

Some people find it more convenient to receive their mail at a post office box in a nearby post office. Post office boxes can be rented by anyone for a monthly fee. You will be able to choose from several box sizes and you will be given a key to your box. In some places, the lobby of the post office, where the post office boxes are located, is open 24 hours a day; in other locations, you will need to collect your mail during the posted hours of operation.

There are several ways to send mail. There is a local post office in virtually every community in the United States where you can take your mail and purchase stamps, services, and mailing supplies. Stamped envelopes can be put in one of the blue mailboxes that dot city and town streets. If you don't see a mailbox on a nearby street corner, you can always find one in front of a post office. Before depositing your mail, be sure you are using the appropriate box—some are marked for express or local mail only.

You can also leave your letters at your own mailbox for the mail carrier to pick up. Be sure that the outgoing mail can be easily seen by the mail carrier. Many people clip their outgoing mail to the outside of the mailbox or tuck the edge of the envelope under the mailbox lid. If you live in a rural area or have a very long driveway, your mailbox may be on a post by the street. These types of mailboxes often have a red flag on the side. Place your mail in the box and raise the flag to indicate that mail needs to be picked up. Many large apartment complexes have a drop box for outgoing mail located near the mailboxes. If you don't see a drop box, ask your mail carrier, the doorman, or your neighbors if there is a designated spot for leaving outgoing mail in the building.

You will see blue mailboxes on many city and neighborhood corners; a sign on the mailbox will tell you the next time mail will be picked up from that box. If there are two mailboxes together, one is probably for express or local mail only; be sure to drop your mail in the correct box. If you need to send a parcel or package or want to take advantage of any supplemental services, such as insured or priority mail, you should take your mail to a post office.

Stamps are readily available in many places as well. For example, many large companies have a stamp vending machine. You will find a vending machine in many transportation hubs, such as airports and central train stations. You can purchase stamps in many grocery and convenience stores, or you can buy them using your credit card from the U.S. Post Office Web site or by telephone; they will arrive in the mail in three to five days.

Other Shipping Services

Other companies offer domestic and international delivery service. These include FedEx, Airborne Express, United Parcel Service (UPS), and DHL Worldwide Express. These companies offer quick and safe delivery of your packages and letters. The range of services offered varies from company to company, but most offer several delivery options and package tracking. You can contact the company directly to find an office or drop-off location near you; some will pick up your package from your home or office. In addition, many cities and towns have businesses that specialize in shipping—they will pack your items and help you fill out the necessary forms. You can find a local shipping business by looking in the yellow pages of your telephone book.

TIPPING

Tipping is common in the United States. People in many professions rely on tips to supplement relatively low wages. In this section, we'll introduce you to some of the most common tipping situations and some guidelines to use when you tip. Of course, people tip because they have received a service; the amount can be increased or decreased according to the quality of service that you receive. And tipping is a personal choice; different people have different rules for tipping. You will find, too, that in large cities, people tend to tip more generously and more frequently. As you can probably imagine, tips in posh hotels and restaurants are usually higher.

Travelers around the world know that tips are the norm in hotels. Porters are usually tipped $1–$2 per bag. If you are staying for several days, you can leave a tip for the maid at the end of your stay (equaling about $1–$2 per day). Some hotels provide an envelope if you wish to tip; you can also leave the money on a table or other convenient place. If the hotel has a doorman or concierge who is particularly helpful, you may want to tip him or her as well. For example, if the doorman cheerfully gets you a cab every morning of your five day stay and helps you load your luggage into the taxi, you may want to give him a few dollars at the end of your stay.

In a bar or restaurant, the waiter or waitress generally receives a 15–20% tip. Bartenders are also tipped around 15–20%. Rather than calculating the exact percentages, most people leave a dollar or two per drink. If you had your food delivered to you from a restaurant, tip about 15%; if the delivery person had to bike through the rain to get your food to you, he or she deserves a little more!

If you have your car parked by a valet (a person hired by an establishment to park guests' cars) or if you park in a full-service garage (where they park your car for you), tip the valet $1–$2. While most people tip the valet after he or she returns the car, some people give him or her some cash when they drop off the car so the valet will be especially careful with, or will keep an eye on, the car.

Taxi drivers are tipped around 10–15%, but this is usually done by rounding up the fare by the appropriate amount; If you have called for car service, the driver generally receives a similar tip. Some people tip the driver of a hotel or an airport shuttle $1–$2. Tip an airport porter or curbside check-in porter $1–$2 per bag; increase the tip if the porter has been especially helpful or if your bags are very heavy or difficult to handle.

There are some people who perform services around your home who are customarily tipped. For example, if you live in an apartment building with a doorman or superintendent, you may want to tip them for performing a special service—or in an attempt to get service! Most people give the people who work in their building an extra cash gift around the Christmas and New Year holidays. There are no hard and fast rules about the amount to give; ask your neighbors to tell you what is customary in your building.

If you live in a suburb, you may have your paper delivered to you daily. Just before Christmas, you are likely to find a holiday greeting card and an empty envelope included with your newspaper—the envelope is for you to tip the carrier. However, you should never tip the mail carrier (he or she is a federal employee and is not allowed to accept tips); other tradespeople, such as plumbers, electricians, meter readers, etc., are also not traditionally given a tip.

When you are ready to move into a new home, you may hire a moving company. Most people tip the movers about $10 per person, although the amount can be increased or decreased depending on how difficult the move was and how much care was taken with your belongings. The same is true for delivery people (except for employees of freight services, such as FedEx or UPS). For example, if the movers had to haul a grand piano into your second-story music room through a window, tip them generously!

Another person you should tip is your hairdresser (anywhere from $2–$20 or more, depending on the cost of your cut; the total is usually around 10–20%); give the person who washes your hair $2–$5 as well.

As you go through your day, you will encounter other people who help you in ways large and small. While it is not mandatory to tip these people, many people do give them a small amount of money, especially if service is rendered willingly and cheerfully. Examples include the person who carries your groceries to the car for you and the person who hand washes or dries your car at the car wash. These are situations where you will use your own judgment on whether or not to tip.

SIX

BUSINESS ENVIRONMENT

Before beginning to do business in the United States, it will be helpful to learn about the American business environment. This section will acquaint you with the basics of business in the United States.

COMPANY VALUES

The basic value of every American company is painfully simple: money. Companies exist to make money. When a company has to choose between its bottom line and its employees, the bottom line wins virtually every time. Newspapers carry stories of massive layoffs at even the most stable of companies. When money is tight, employees feel the pinch professionally and personally, since extras, such as training and bonuses, are generally the first things to disappear from the budget.

The evolution of the American economy has led to an atmosphere where neither the employer nor the employee feels any great loyalty to each other. Companies have no reservations about laying off employees when times are tough. By the same token, an employee may accept a job at a company with the intention of working there for a few years to gain experience before moving on to a more lucrative position in another company. Money is a huge motivator to both sides: the company wants to keep a favorable financial position and keep the shareholders happy, and the employees want to maximize their personal incomes. This has led to a relatively unstable workforce with high turnover as both employer and employee focus on the all-important aspect of business: money.

Despite the focus on financial gain, many companies do have programs in place to contribute to their communities in various ways. For example, most companies make substantial contributions to charity. (The company is fully aware of the tax break it will receive for contributing to a charity.) Your company may match your donation to a charity, or it may have other programs in place to encourage employees to volunteer their time.

Even though many employees do not feel a bond of loyalty to their employers, Americans in general have a strong work ethic, traits handed down both from the Puritan settlers and from immigrants from all walks of life who came to America with little else but a dream and the will to make it come true. As a result, hard work is something that is valued, and a person who works hard for his or her success, fame, or fortune is admired more than someone to whom these things were handed.

Many Americans work long hours and tend to place an inherent value on working for work's sake. As a result, they often have the expectation that others work as long and as late as they do. This can lead to conflicts when Americans encounter people from cultures that value family and personal time over work. Many Americans stereotype such people as lazy.

COMPANY STRUCTURE

There are five main types of company structures in the United States: sole proprietorship, general partnership, limited partnership, corporation, and limited liability company (LLC). The following paragraphs provide a brief overview of the different types of company structures.

The first three types of company structures—sole proprietorship, general partnership, and limited partnership—provide the benefit of exemption from double taxation, since a separate entity is not formed. There are higher risks, however, as the owners are liable for the debts of the company. Corporations protect owners from personal liability, but they are subject to taxes as separate entities, while the last type of corporate structure, a limited liability company, is a hybrid that seeks to provide the best of both worlds.

Sole Proprietorship

A sole proprietorship is the simplest business structure and does not involve the formation of a separate legal entity. In a sole proprietorship, the business owner is liable for all of the business actions and debts.

General Partnership

A general partnership is like a sole proprietorship in many ways, but it allows for two or more people to go into business together. Like a sole proprietorship, a general partnership does not require the creation of a separate legal entity, and the owners or partners remain liable for all business actions and debts. A general partnership does require more paperwork in the form of formal partnership agreements specifying income allocation and business continuity plans in the event of a partner's death or departure from the business.

Limited Partnership

A limited partnership consists of one or more general partners and one or more limited partners. Although the general partner(s) have unlimited liability, the liability of the limited partner(s) is restricted to the amount of the initial investment, as long as they do not have an active role in the business operations.

Corporation

Forming a corporation requires that a Certificate or Articles of Incorporation be filed with the state government where the corporation is based, creating a separate legal entity. The corporation must have a board of directors and corporate officers. The corporate structure makes it easier to have many owners in the company through the sale of shares. The liability of the owners is limited, but the company is taxed separately from the owners.

Limited Liability Company (LLC)

The limited liability company, or LLC, is a relatively new option for business owners. It provides limited liability for the owners and avoids double taxation. However, because it is a relatively new form of business ownership, some states have not fully developed regulations regarding LLCs, and even the federal Internal Revenue Service (IRS) could make some changes in their treatment of these businesses.

BUSINESS HOURS

The phrase used most often to describe a typical workweek is "nine to five," but this phrase does not apply to everyone. Office hours vary, and there is a growing number of people who work more than the standard 40 hours a week. It is therefore difficult to categorize typical business hours in the United States, but here are some general guidelines.

Many companies do list office hours that reflect the standard, such as 9:00 AM to 5:00 PM. This is generally when you will find the reception area open to receive visitors. Behind the internal doors, however, you would find many people working until 6:00, 7:00, or

8:00 PM on a regular basis and sometimes longer when there is a special need, such as an important deadline or a crisis at hand. The general perception is that the lower-level employees, such as the receptionist, administrative assistants, clerks, etc., will leave promptly at the end of the work day while mid- and upper-level employees, such as managers, will stay as late as necessary to get done what needs to be done. Some industries, such as investment banking and advertising, are notorious for expecting employees to work well into the night and even on weekends if the workload warrants it.

There are many exceptions to this rule. For a variety of reasons, much of the American workforce works outside of the nine-to-five parameters. For example, if a company has a customer service department, they may have extended hours every day or a few days a week. They may even be open on the weekend to accommodate the needs of their customers. Other companies have some departments that are open 24 hours a day, 7 days a week. The people who work during those times are generally in support positions, such as technical support for computers, or work in global companies that must accommodate the business hours of clients and offices around the world.

And, of course, there are many industries and occupations that require employees to work other shifts as well. Hospitals and law enforcement agencies can't simply shut down at night. Manufacturing facilities also often run 24 hours a day, creating a need for three shifts of workers. Retail stores are often open until 9:00 or 10:00 PM, and restaurants and bars are open even later.

Many industries have extended their hours to maximize their production and to accommodate the needs of consumers. Banking, however, is one industry that has not. Although some bank branches are open until 5:00 PM, many bank branches close at 3:00 or 4:00 in the afternoon. You may find a bank that has extended hours one day a week or that is open on Saturday morning, but those remain rare. Banks have sought to meet their customers' 24-hour needs through other means, such as ATMs and online banking.

No matter what hours you work, you are entitled to breaks throughout the day. Lunch breaks are anywhere from half an hour to an hour, depending on the company's policies. In an office, most people go to lunch between 12:00 and 2:00 PM. Some people work through their lunch hours, eating at their desks while they work. And although you may be allowed other breaks (generally 15 minutes for every four hours worked), it is more common for people to leave their desks for only a few minutes to grab a cup of coffee or step outside to smoke a cigarette.

THE AMERICAN WORK WEEK AND BENEFITS

The standard workweek is 40 hours, although many people work more. In recent years, many companies have begun to experiment with alternatives to the regular 40-hour week. Ideas like working from home for part of the week, flexible hours, and job sharing have been implemented to balance the demands of the workforce with the needs of the company.

Benefits, such as paid vacation time, health care, and retirement benefits, can be offered at the discretion of your employer. Most medium and large corporations have found that a good benefits package is an essential part of attracting and retaining employees. Your human resources department or manager can help you find the information you need about benefits offered by your company.

Vacation benefits vary from company to company, but your vacation allotment generally increases with your years of service. For example, when you are first employed, you may get only one week of paid vacation during your first year on the job. After three years you may get two weeks of vacation, after five years you may get three weeks. Generally speaking, higher-level jobs come with more benefits, such as more vacation time, but there is usually a cap at four weeks.

Most companies have a holiday calendar that matches that of the federal government, allowing for up to 11 paid holidays for most employees. In addition, many companies allow their employees to take one or two personal days per year. These are paid days off that the employee can take whenever he or she likes. Many people choose to take a personal day in conjunction with a regular holiday to extend their time off, such as the Friday after Thanksgiving, or to observe a non-Christian religious day, such as Yom Kippur.

Health insurance is essential in the United States; the cost of medical care is astronomical. Employers can get better rates for a group of employees than you can get for yourself individually. The depth and breadth of insurance coverage depends on your company. For example, you may have to pay for supplemental dental, vision, or prescription medicine insurance, or you may be limited in your choices of insurance plans. However, it is common for an employer to offer some choice in insurance plans (HMO, PPO, etc.), including plans that cover the families of employees. The employer will often bear some of the cost of the insurance. (See the "Insurance" section of the "Living and Staying in the United States" chapter for an overview of medical insurance.)

Retirement benefits also vary, but many companies give their employees the option of making contributions to retirement accounts directly from their paychecks. The money contributed to these accounts can often be deducted before taxes, reducing the amount of your income that is taxed. In addition, many companies will match a certain percentage of your contributions. Some common retirement plans include 401(k), 403(b), IRA (Individual Retirement Account), and Keogh accounts. Each of them fills a specific need and there are criteria that apply to each. Your company's benefits department can tell you which, if any, plans are available to you. Of course, if your stay in the United States is temporary, you will need to determine if these types of investments fit your retirement strategy; a financial planner can help you make that decision.

Employees receive either an annual salary or an hourly wage. Your paycheck will include many deductions, starting with federal income tax, which everyone must pay. Some states and cities also have an income tax. For example, workers in New York City pay federal, state, and city income taxes. Employees in Florida, however, pay only a federal income tax, since Florida does not have a state income tax.

Employees are also required to contribute to Social Security and Medicare (these deductions are often listed together as "FICA" [Federal Insurance Contributions Act]) and to disability insurance. Other deductions depend on the benefits offered by your employer. For example, your health insurance and retirement benefit payments are usually deducted directly from your paycheck.

OFFICE SPACE

A floor plan of a typical American office closely resembles a labyrinth or maze. Americans value their privacy and independence, so most offices are laid out with cubicles, separated by chest-high partitions, filling the interior spaces; private offices line the outsides. Your relative rank is evident in your workspace. For example, secretaries often have a desk or partial cubicle outside of their boss's office. Other support staff may have partial or shared cubicles, and those a bit higher may have their own cubicles. Private offices are coveted, since only the highest-ranking employees receive them.

In office buildings where there are more private offices than cubicles, your status is indicated by the size and location of your workspace. Large offices with windows mean that you are higher on the totem pole than your colleagues whose smaller, windowless offices are in the center.

Generally speaking, most companies try to encourage efficiency and internal communication by keeping the people who work together located in the same general vicinity. Departments or permanent teams generally sit together, and managers usually have their cubicles or offices near their subordinates. In many companies, the executive offices are all located in one area, often on or near the top floor of the building, and are usually more opulently furnished than the rest of the building.

In keeping with the informal atmosphere in most offices, people often make their workspaces more comfortable with pictures of their families, plants, comic strips cut from a newspaper, souvenirs from their travels, and other knickknacks. Although you are free to decorate as you wish, you do not often see diplomas on the wall except in professions that require certification, such as medicine or law; it can be regarded as arrogant or boastful if a manager displays his or her diploma. In most offices, it is perfectly acceptable to keep a coffee cup on your desk and to eat at your desk if you wish. (Note that some companies have specific policies about workspace appearances, such as rules that prohibit employees from tacking anything on their cubicle walls; your coworkers or the human resources department can tell you if there are rules you need to observe.)

Most people keep their office doors open unless they are in a meeting or on a telephone call and do not wish to be disturbed. For some people, a closed door usually indicates a desire for privacy and is not a definitive "do not disturb" sign. This varies from person to person, but you will soon learn if your colleagues can be interrupted when their office doors are closed. If you do need to speak to someone whose door is closed, etiquette dictates that you knock first. Even when a person's door is open, most people will generally knock on the doorframe or otherwise get the occupant's attention before entering the office. In most offices, you don't need to wait for an invitation to sit down or pull up a chair. In all instances, it is best, when in doubt, to follow the lead of your coworkers.

AN INFORMAL ATMOSPHERE

In most workplaces, you will find an atmosphere in keeping with the general American inclination toward informality. Observers from some cultures have wondered how Americans ever get anything done, since they never seem to be at their desks. Information is exchanged in hallways, by the coffee machine, and in the break room as well as in meetings and other more formal conduits.

Your coworkers will greet you casually in the morning with a "Good morning," "Hey," or even just a smile or nod. Handshakes are generally reserved for meetings with clients or people whom you rarely see. These brief casual exchanges continue throughout the day as you pass people in the halls or see them in the cafeteria.

Interruptions are frequent as people stop by your desk or call with a question. Meetings often happen without much warning, and most people just call or stop by a colleague's office rather than make a formal appointment. Even appointments with colleagues are informally made and are subject to change. For example, you might get a brief e-mail from a coworker asking if you are free in about 10 minutes to discuss a project you are working on together.

The informal tone is present in meetings, e-mails, and other written communications as well. Of course, when the meeting is particularly important, such as a first meeting with a potential client or a serious communication, more formality is called for, but you will find that most business relationships quickly move from a formal to an informal tone.

HECTIC PACE

American business environments may be informal, but business is conducted at a hectic speed. Most planning is short term and there always seems to be a deadline looming. Communications fly back and forth rapidly, and you are expected to reply to your telephone calls and e-mails promptly. The phrases "ASAP" (as soon as possible; this phrase is said either by spelling it out—A-S-A-P—or as "ay sap") and "I need this yesterday" (this is not a grammatical error, but an expression that means "This is already late and I need it more urgently than ASAP") are consistently found in all types of communications. (See the "Business Communication" section of "Business Step-by-Step" for more information on responding to telephone messages and e-mail.)

You will see this urgency everywhere, even in the packages you ship. Getting something to someone in three to five days will no longer suffice. Shippers such as FedEx, UPS, DHL, and others have in recent years increased their service to offer two-day, overnight, and even next-morning service.

PERSONAL SPACE

Differences in our need for personal space can cause tension, although we may not know why. Trivial as it may seem, it can be an important, albeit unconscious, part of our assessment of each other. If you watch two Americans having a conversation, you would note that they keep each other at arm's length—literally. Americans are most comfortable when the other person is about three feet away from them. Any closer and Americans feel encroached upon and are likely to think that the other person is being pushy. This is a marked contrast to the personal space needs of many other cultures. Newcomers from countries where people require less personal space often get a feeling that their American speaking partners are cold, distant, or uninterested in them. The person with the smaller bubble of personal space tries to close the gap while the American backs up, making for an interesting dance around the room, but creating discomfort for both people, even if the reason isn't obvious.

Of course, the opposite is true as well. If you require more space than the typical American, you might feel that a conversation partner is crowding you and will attempt to back away. In these instances, it is the American who comes across as pushy and who feels that you are uninterested. In either case, if you try to be conscious of your environment, you should become aware of the times that personal space is causing tension; you will soon adapt to the American need for space and will be more comfortable with your colleagues.

THE AMERICAN WORKFORCE

Jobs in the United States are generally characterized as blue-collar or white-collar. Blue-collar workers are those who are manual laborers; white-collar workers are office workers, sales people, managers, teachers, and others whose jobs do not include manual labor. In today's workforce, white-collar workers outnumber blue-collar workers, and this trend is on the rise as service sectors continue to grow in relation to manufacturing.

Unions

Union activity began in the United States in the late 18th century, as craftsmen sought to uphold the standards of their craft and prevent employers from hiring untrained laborers and importing foreign labor. The history of American labor unions has had many ups and downs. Labor unions were instrumental in passing legislation, such as the Fair Labor Standards Act and the Social Security Act. However, unions suffered setbacks at various times, as their leaders were accused of everything from misuse of union funds to extortion and espionage. Unions thrived during the Depression of the 1930s, but membership has been on a steady decline since World War II. In the 1960s, union members represented 30% of the workforce; today it is just below 14%. This decline can be traced in part to the changing landscape of the American workforce. Service industries, traditionally more reluctant to unionize, have grown substantially while manufacturing, the power base of unions, has declined.

Unions are organized in two ways: by craft (e.g., International Brotherhood of Carpenters and Joiners) or by industry, (e.g., Hotel Employees and Restaurant Employees International Union, a union whose membership includes every worker in the industry regardless of position). Unions seek to ensure that their members' jobs are secure and that they are receiving appropriate wages and benefits. Many unions have had to take a more conciliatory stance in the face of foreign competition and the shift to a more service-based economy. In fact, by 1996, strikes had reached a 50-year low. However, unions continue to play an important role in employee relations in some companies and industries, and their actions can affect us all—just ask anyone who was grounded by the Air Controllers Strike in 1981 or who was unable to get their packages delivered when UPS held a strike in 1997.

A Diverse Workforce

The American workforce is a diverse one, mirroring the portrait of America itself. Your colleagues will be of every race and religion. This diversity has enriched the workforce, bringing together a wide variety of people, but it has also led to difficulties. Laws have been enacted to protect workers against discrimination on the basis of race, gender, religion, age, and disability. Although America has come a long way from the days of segregation, in reality, discrimination still exists.

Many companies and organizations have instituted awareness training for their employees to increase their understanding of one another and to help create an environment that embraces diversity.

WOMEN IN BUSINESS

According to the Department of Labor, 99 out of 100 women will work for pay at some point in their lives. Women currently make up about half of the workforce, and the number of working women is growing steadily. Despite the major role that women play in the workforce, their wages are generally lower than the wages paid to men in the same jobs; women are paid about 75% of what men make.

Women in the United States work for many reasons. In some instances, the woman may be a single mother who is the sole earner for the family. In other cases, a single income is not enough to support the family, so both spouses work. And, of course, whether they have children or not, some women work because they want to; they are stimulated by their careers and enjoy the challenges that their jobs bring.

The move of women away from the role of housewife and homemaker to working mother has brought with it much controversy and has raised many questions for women who seek to do it all: have a family and a career. While men have increasingly taken on a greater role in raising children and doing household chores, some women remain the primary caregivers for children and continue to be responsible for running the household. This has created pressure for these women to be "superwomen," women who work full time yet still manage to keep their homes and families running smoothly. Unfortunately, there never seem to be enough hours in the day to excel at either, and these women feel that they fall short of the "superwoman" ideal. Consequently, they feel guilty about their need or desire to work at the expense of spending time with their children. Still, the "superwoman" ideal is gradually being erased as more men begin to participate in child care and housework, allowing their partners more flexibility to act as workers without the stress of being solely responsible for what goes on at home.

In the workplace, American women expect to be treated the same as their male colleagues in business. They expect that their ideas and input be treated with the same weight and that they receive the same opportunities.

Despite the many advances in equality in the workplace, there are still glass ceilings, barriers to the highest levels of management that are very difficult to break through. It remains a fact that the majority of power in business remains in the hands of men, and much business is done through a network of connections that are not easily accessible to women. There are many women in management positions, but they remain outnumbered by men, and the higher the rank, the fewer women you will find. Women hold about 44% of management, executive, and administrative jobs, yet occupy fewer than 5% of top-level executive positions. However, this is slowly changing as more women break through the glass ceilings and create opportunities for other women to follow in their footsteps.

Unlike their counterparts in some cultures who have preferred to work behind the scenes, American women have approached the issue of gender equality head on and very aggressively, openly demanding equal rights with demonstrations, marches, and vocal appearances in public forums. While this has brought about relatively swift changes, it has also brought criticism. Some feel threatened by feminism and seek to blame America's societal woes on women who are not happy with their roles. Others feel that women have traded their defining traits of femininity for equality.

Sexual Harrassment

No matter what your personal feelings are about women in business, you must remember that the legal system protects women against discrimination or sexual harassment. Social courtesies aside, there are some behaviors that are absolutely inappropriate—and illegal—in the workplace. The spotlight has recently been on sexual harassment, which is illegal. Sexual harassment can encompass many things, and situations are not always black and white. At the furthest extreme, sexual harassment is when your boss refuses to promote you or give you a raise unless you have sexual intercourse with him (or her, in the case of a male subordinate). Less well-defined, but still illegal, are instances where a hostile work environment exists. This can be where one or more coworkers make sexual innuendos, tell inappropriate jokes, or have inappropriate physical contact with coworkers. In general, you should never feel uncomfortable in your workplace because you are a woman. If you encounter circumstances that make you uncomfortable, you can speak with your supervisor or with a human resources representative. The best way to ensure that the work place is free from sexual harassment is to keep your interactions with coworkers on a professional level. No matter what your gender, flirting and provocative behavior are inappropriate in the business environment.

Tips for Women in Business

Whether you are a man or a woman, your appearance is important and impacts the way you will be perceived. Certain industries, such as entertainment and fashion, have an environment where personal creativity and flair can be expressed in the way you dress; others, such as banking or finance, have an implicit requirement that you dress more conservatively. Some companies have a casual dress policy while others require employees to maintain a more formal, corporate appearance. Make sure that what you wear is within the guidelines set by your company or organization.

Within the boundaries of your company's rules, women may dress how they please. There is a wide range of styles to choose from when it comes to a work wardrobe. Women wear both slacks and dresses or skirts to work; business suits may have either a skirt or pants. However, it is inappropriate to dress in a sexy or provocative manner at work. Even if short skirts are all the rage, you should avoid wearing very short skirts or dresses to work. Heavy makeup and excessive jewelry are also unsuitable for the workplace. In general, you will want your wardrobe to be similar to that of your male coworkers, in level of formality if not in style. In other words, if you are going to a meeting with an important client, and your male team members are wearing suits, you will probably want to wear a suit as well.

The movement to equality in the workplace has led to some confusion in the area of etiquette. To be honest, both men and women are somewhat unsure how to blend social and business etiquette. For example, if a man would not rise when a male colleague entered the room, should he rise for a female colleague? Should a man hold the door for a female colleague or not? This sometimes leads to awkwardness for everyone when both reach for the doorknob. There are no hard and fast answers to these questions. As a woman in business, you should be prepared to accept, but not expect, social courtesies, such as entering the elevator door first or having men pull out your chair at a restaurant.

SEVEN

BUSINESS STEP-BY-STEP

Now that we've looked at the overall structure and atmosphere of business in the United States, let's take a look at the specifics of doing business in America.

Americans have a reputation of being quite informal when it comes to business. While this is generally true, there are many factors that can influence the level of formality of any given situation. Certain industries, such as advertising or entertainment, are less formal than others. Younger employees are usually less formal than the previous generation; newer companies are less formal than older, more established companies. The nature of the interaction, such as a conversation between two colleagues versus an important negotiation, also determines the level of formality. Therefore, it is best to define the formality involved in American business on a case-by-case basis. As a general rule you can begin by being more formal and taking your cues from colleagues and clients on when to move to a more informal level. By doing so you are showing respect, not taking liberties that aren't necessarily granted, and avoiding offense. Your American colleagues will let you know if and when a more relaxed atmosphere is appropriate.

APPOINTMENTS

A day planner is an important accessory for most business people. It is used to keep track of meetings and tasks that need to be done. If you want to have someone's full attention, your name needs to be in that person's planner, preferably in ink.

When you want to meet with a client or contact, it is essential to make an appointment—and to arrive on time; this holds true for telephone conferences as well as in-person meetings. If you are going to be more than 5 or 10 minutes late, it's advisable to call to let the person know you are running late; luckily, the widespread use of cellular phones makes that easy to do. If you need to cancel an appointment, give as much notice as you can. Of course, people do understand that delays happen sometimes, but a person who consistently cancels appointments or arrives late is usually viewed as unprofessional.

It's generally not necessary to make appointments with coworkers, but if you have an important matter to discuss, you may want to ask your colleague to mark you down on his or her calendar.

BUSINESS CARDS

Business cards are an important part of doing business in the United States, but they are used more for the purpose of exchanging information than for establishing status. Business cards are passed around freely, and someone who has given you a card before may offer you another card when you meet again. Cards are treated casually; you will see people giving them a cursory glance when they receive them, jotting notes on them, and immediately stowing them

in their wallet. Business cards can also be distributed at social occasions to potential business contacts or simply to give someone your contact information. If you are in a position to meet a lot of people, especially clients and contacts outside of your own company, you will want to keep a quantity of business cards at hand.

Business cards represent the image that the business or organization wants to project. Therefore, the business card of a graphic arts company is likely to be splashier than that of a more established, staid corporation.

A typical business card includes the company's logo and the individual's name, title, and contact information, such as telephone and fax numbers and mail and e-mail addresses. Most business people do not include any reference to their university degrees. Two exceptions to this are medical professionals, who place MD (Medical Doctor), DDS (Doctor of Dental Science or Surgery), or other appropriate letters after their names, and college or university professors, who often put PhD after their names.

DRESSING FOR SUCCESS

Most companies have a dress policy, which you can get from your company's human resources department. Your company's policy may offer specific guidelines, letting you know that jeans, t-shirts and sandals are not appropriate at any time, or it may be more general, stating only that employees are expected to dress appropriately. However, you will quickly learn from observing your coworkers what the office standards are.

In offices where professional dress is required, men should wear business suits and ties. There isn't as much personal flair in men's business clothing in the United States as there is in other countries. The palette for men's suits tends to be subdued: darker blues and grays, olive greens, etc. Although tans and some other lighter colors are not inappropriate for warmer weather, summer suits are generally defined by the weight of the material, not by the color. You will see pinstripes and subtle checked patterns, but in general, both the colors and the styles are subdued; no matter how well-cut, your colleagues will probably look askance if you show up in a mustard yellow or purple suit. Self-expression for businessmen, therefore, tends to appear only in neckties.

Women have greater latitude in business attire. Women can wear suits with skirts, suits with slacks, or dresses. For meetings with clients outside of the office, many women prefer to wear a business suit that is comparable to those worn by male coworkers rather than a dress or skirt-and-jacket ensemble. Women also have a wider range of colors from which to choose. They should, however, be careful that they do not dress in a provocative manner: low-cut blouses, short skirts, and shoes with five-inch heels are inappropriate. Pantyhose or stockings are part of a woman's business ensemble, even in summer.

Many offices that continue to require business attire have instituted "casual Fridays." This means that on Fridays, employees can wear casual clothes. The definition of casual varies from business casual to allowing jeans and t-shirts.

The standard business casual costume is slacks or khakis (chinos) and a shirt or blouse with a collar for both men and women. Many men choose to wear slacks with a business shirt, minus the coat and tie; women often wear slacks or skirts and blouses instead of suits. More and more offices are adopting this more casual standard of everyday dress, even in industries that have traditionally been more conservative.

At the furthest extreme are companies that are completely casual. These are usually young companies with young employees as well as certain industries, such as publishing, music, and fashion. Their philosophy is that you will be more productive if you are comfortable, and employees are permitted to wear jeans, t-shirts, and shorts—practically anything short of a pair of pajamas.

Of course, no matter what you wear to the office on a regular basis, there will be times when you will want to dress up or down. For example, if you are going to visit a client, you will probably want to wear a business suit. Business entertaining and business/social occasions also call for a wardrobe review: Lunch with an important client or with your boss may require a business suit, while the company's annual summer barbeque means something more casual. If you are ever in doubt about what is appropriate to wear, you can ask a colleague or friend for advice.

BUSINESS COMMUNICATION

Information tends to flow freely in most American organizations, so you will be inundated with communiqués from every direction and in every form: telephone messages, e-mail, faxes, and mail.

Only at the upper echelons do people have a secretary or an assistant to screen their telephone calls, mail, or e-mail. Most people answer their own phones and read and respond to their own e-mail.

Business communication is fairly informal and very frequent, especially with the advent of computers and cellular phones. Telephones have red lights that tell you if you have a voice mail waiting, and your computer lets you know when you receive an e-mail. Being out of the office is no longer a valid excuse for not responding to communication. If you look around you on the street or in the subway, you'll see that more and more people have cellular phones and PDAs (personal digital assistants—small, handheld devices that allow you to send and receive e-mail, access the Internet, keep track of your appointments, and more). You are expected to respond promptly to all types of communication, usually within 24 hours, if not sooner. Even if you receive a request that you cannot immediately fulfill, it is common practice to reply to the sender confirming that you received the message and letting them know when you can fulfill their request.

Americans like to be kept informed, and they have many ways of doing this. E-mail has become an integral part of American business, since it allows for easy, inexpensive dissemination of information. E-mail software allows you to create a distribution list to easily send the same message to many people; some voice mail systems have a similar feature.

Also popular are FYIs. This stands for "for your information;" if you receive something that says "FYI," you do not have to respond, but you are expected to read it and file the information away, even if only mentally. People frequently use the cc (carbon copy) or bcc (blind carbon copy) feature of their e-mail software. This allows them to target one person with the message and inform other people at the same time. (You should note that ccs are sometimes also used as a weapon: By adding someone's boss in the cc list, you are implicitly saying "Now your boss knows about it, so you'd better take swift action.")

Many people have written e-mails in anger or frustration or have criticized a fellow employee, only to regret it when the e-mail fell into the wrong hands. Expect that your e-mail will be forwarded to the people whom the recipient thinks need to read it or will reply to it, adding a cc or bcc. Would you like it if you read through an e-mail that had been forwarded around the office and back, only to find at the very bottom, buried in a reply to a reply to a reply, a criticism of yourself? Even if you mark something as confidential, the best rule of thumb is to expect that it will be read by the one person you don't want to see it and choose your language accordingly. In fact, if you have something to say that you don't want others to read, consider an alternate form of communication, such as an in-person conversation.

E-mail Tips

- Keep your messages short and to the point. This is true for both voice mail messages and e-mails.
- Limit your e-mails to one point as much as possible. People are much more likely to read and process a concise, one-item e-mail than a long one that addresses several points simultaneously.
- Keep social conversation to a minimum. For example, a typical routine e-mail message to a colleague may start with "Hi, [name]" and immediately launch into the reason for the e-mail. A more casual e-mail or voice mail may go on to say something like "How's it going?", but there will rarely be much more than that in a business communication.
- Be mindful of the content of your e-mail. Most companies have policies that prohibit employees from sending or forwarding e-mails containing racial or sexual remarks; doing so can get you fired.

GIFT-GIVING

Gift-giving does not play a major role in American business relation-ships. The American mentality regards the giving of gifts of value as bribery, a practice that is contrary to the American preference for merit-based business practices. Because bribery is also illegal, both at home and abroad, it is important to be conscious of the boundary between giving a gift and bribery. Therefore, business gifts tend to be of token value and are generally not given as an inducement to begin a business relationship.

Occasions calling for gifts are also limited. If your company has recently forged a joint venture with another company, the teams that negotiated the deal might be presented with a token, such as a small acrylic plaque etched with both companies' logos, to mark the occasion. You might also give them small items carrying the company logo, such as pens, paperweights, or tote bags. These types of items are also given away at trade shows and at other events. On a higher level are items such as tickets to sporting and cultural events; many larger companies purchase blocks of tickets that can be given to important clients. Generally speaking, it is inappropriate to give gifts of a higher value; your company can provide you with specific information on its gift giving guidelines.

If you are invited to someone's home for a business/social gathering, you should take a gift for your hosts. Appropriate gifts for such occasions are a bottle of wine or a bouquet of flowers; for a more formal gathering, you may want to have a floral arrangement delivered to your hosts or bring a bottle of liquor, such as brandy or scotch.

With few exceptions, you will not be expected to give gifts to coworkers. In many offices, people choose to mark special occasions in the lives of coworkers with a small gift. If someone in the office is getting married, having a baby, or retiring, his or her coworkers may chip in to buy an appropriate gift. Because many people are contributing, the individual amounts are usually small, around $5–$10. One person will generally take charge of collecting contributions and purchasing a gift and card, which everyone signs.

In most places, birthdays are not celebrated in the office. If the people in your office are especially close, someone may suggest collecting money for a gift. However, this is generally too complex—and birthdays occur too often—to be practical. In some offices, a birthday card signed by everyone in the office may be the norm, or there may be a monthly mini-party, with cake and sodas, that includes everyone who had a birthday that month.

There are two days that may be celebrated in your office: Administrative Professionals Day (formerly known as Secretaries Day) and Christmas.

The last full week in April is Administrative Professionals week, with Wednesday being Administrative Professionals Day. This observance is designed to recognize the contribution of all support staff, not just secretaries. At some point during this week, bosses generally give their administrative staff some type of gift; if the staff supports multiple people, they often get together to give the gift. Traditional gifts are lunch at a nice restaurant and having a bouquet of flowers delivered. You can be creative, as long as the gift is not too personal. For example, you could give a subscription to a professional magazine or pay for the employee to register in a seminar that will develop his or her skills.

It is not uncommon for coworkers to exchange gifts at Christmas, but these are almost always small gifts, such as a Christmas ornament, a scented candle, or even homemade cookies. Unfortunately, there are no hard and fast rules for this exchange. Of course, you are not obligated to give gifts to your coworkers, even if someone gives you one. You can ask your colleagues what the custom is in your office.

In some offices, there is a more structured gift exchange, often called "Secret Santa." Participation is not mandatory, but if you choose to participate, you will draw a coworker's name at random, or be assigned one. You will then buy a gift for that person, but the gift is given anonymously and you sign the tag or card "From your Secret Santa." There is usually a limit on the amount of money you can spend on the gift, such as $10 or $15.

BUSINESS ENTERTAINING

Business entertaining plays a relatively minor role in the United States. First-time visitors on a business trip are often surprised to find that they are largely left to fend for themselves when the meetings are over. There are many contributing factors to this practice. A successful American business relationship is not dependent on a corresponding personal relationship, and the general American attitude of "time is money" inhibits a lot of companies from entertaining visitors. For example, a business person who has traveled to another city for business purposes has probably crammed as many appointments into his or her schedule as possible to maximize the value of the trip. Indeed, he or she may have taken an early-morning flight and be on a return flight at the end of the day. Such a hectic schedule leaves little room for socializing.

Business lunches are common enough, but are generally less social and more professional in nature. Although there will be some social conversation, it will be overshadowed by the business conversation that never really ended at the office door. Business lunches are usually more than the quick bite to eat that most people call their daily lunch, but they are not lengthy; you are unlikely to spend more than one hour at lunch, and it is often less.

Not as common as the business lunch is the power breakfast, which enjoyed a brief period of popularity in the 1980s. Although power breakfasts are certainly not extinct, they are not as common as the business lunch. People on business trips, for example, might suggest an early-morning meeting at their hotel so that you can begin your business discussion over breakfast.

Business dinners are even less common. A dinner may be scheduled to celebrate a particularly significant occasion, such as the completion of a major venture. For example, if an American company is hosting visitors from another country who are in town for several days while working out the details of a joint venture, the hosting team may invite their guests to dinner. But, like business lunches, business dinners often include both business and social topics and are usually not lengthy affairs.

Business entertaining also appears in the form of intracompany socializing. A team leader might invite his or her team for a weekend barbeque or a Friday night dinner, or a company executive might host a holiday party or occasional dinner party.

Tips for Business Entertaining

- Business entertaining is usually done in restaurants, although you may occasionally be invited to someone's home. If you are going to someone's home, follow the same rules of etiquette that are appropriate for social gatherings.
- When it comes to paying for the meal, be sure to treat your male and female colleagues alike. If your female colleague indi-

cates that she will pay for the meal, let her; thank her for the meal and do not insist on paying.

- Lunch with a business colleague is usually more business than social. Your lunch companion(s) may continually steer the conversation back to business.
- Americans generally do not drink alcohol during business hours. If you are invited to a business lunch, consider foregoing beer or wine for iced tea or a soft drink.
- Even if a business dinner is billed as a social event, expect to hear business discussed throughout the evening.
- Spouses are generally not included in business dinners but may be invited to social/business dinners, especially if they are at someone's home. If you are not sure, you can ask a colleague to clarify whether or not your spouse or a date is included in the invitation. If your spouse is traveling with you on a business trip, it is okay to inquire if he or she can join you at a business dinner so he or she does not have to dine alone.
- If you are visiting the United States, do not expect that your American hosts will have any plans for your time after business hours. Expect to be largely left to your own devices for dinner and any extra days you spend in the area.
- Be on time for all events, business or social.
- A thank-you note or a phone call following a social event is appropriate and appreciated; unfortunately, this practice is not always followed by Americans.

MEETINGS

Many things are accomplished by way of meetings, such as the dissemination of information, setting goals, keeping track of progress, brainstorming, or idea generation. Meetings can take many forms, such as impromptu meetings among a few people, regularly scheduled team or project meetings, or ad hoc meetings. In almost all instances, everyone is allowed to voice an opinion—and everyone is expected to participate.

Americans like agendas, but are willing to deviate from them. Many people take notes on the topics discussed in the meeting, and often there is one person responsible for distributing a brief written summary of the meeting afterward, especially if there are actions to be taken.

Being an Active Meeting Participant

Being an active participant in a meeting means not only listening attentively but speaking up as well. Many teams have regular meetings when each person gives a brief update on his or her activities. However, in other meetings, participants are expected to openly make suggestions and discuss ideas. Although no one is particularly fond of having his or her ideas shot down in public, you are expected to be able to separate criticism of your idea from criticism of yourself. Therefore, if you make a suggestion, you must be prepared for your colleagues to immediately discuss why the idea will or will not work. And if it is something that you believe in, you will have to join in the discussion to defend your idea.

If you wait until after the meeting to approach people individually with your suggestions or opinions, you will often find that the opportunity has passed. Because Americans make decisions, assign tasks, and take action in meetings, it may be too late to offer a new idea, voice a dissenting opinion, or make an alternative suggestion. In fact, you may find that your colleagues respond by saying, "I wish you had brought that up in the meeting." The general feeling may be that you have inconvenienced everyone, since the whole thing must now be revisited.

If this style of participation is not comfortable to you, it can help to prepare ahead of time. For example, if you have an idea, you can write down what you want to say so that you will be able to make your points clearly and concisely.

Of course, this is not possible in situations where a spontaneous response is required. Unfortunately, there is no easy way to prepare for the time when your boss turns to you in a meeting and says, "So, what do *you* think?" When that happens, all you can do is answer honestly, remembering that Americans appreciate directness, whether positive or negative.

NEGOTIATING AND PERSUADING

As a rule, Americans are quite competitive. This begins at an early age, when many children participate in competitive sports, and continues into adulthood as they compete for recognition, reward and promotion. It is also a part of negotiations, both formal and informal. Despite the fact that most people pay lip service to the idea of a "win-win" negotiation that ends in a deal that is beneficial to both parties, most people prefer to triumph over their opponent. This can be done in various ways and does not necessarily imply that the other side loses. It does, however, mean that the negotiator has forced concessions from the other side. Practically speaking, this simply means that both sides approach the negotiating table with three pieces of information in mind: their best-case scenario, what they expect to get, and the absolute least that they can accept. Therefore, a seller who goes into a meeting with a potential buyer may first offer a relatively high price; the buyer, in turn, counters with a very low price. They then will barter back and forth on the price until they reach a price that is acceptable to both or decide that reaching an agreement is not possible. Even when there is little possibility to negotiate price, there is often room to negotiate in other areas, such as delivery date, co-marketing, or development budget, and so on.

Americans typically have a substantial amount of decision-making authority at low to mid levels. You can expect that the person sitting across the negotiating table has the power to make a decision about the matter at hand—and he or she expects the same from you. While some negotiations certainly require consultation with one's superiors, most routine negotiations can be finalized quickly. You will find that your American counterparts become impatient if you do not have the authority to make the decision and must delay while you present the offer to your superiors for a decision; they might even ask if the decision maker can be a part of the negotiation to facilitate closing the deal if they feel that the process is taking too much time.

Americans are more task-oriented than relationship-oriented. When they come to the negotiating table, they are there to make a deal, not to build a relationship. They expect that the negotiations can be concluded quickly and efficiently. This means that they spend little time getting to know you or your company and move right into discussing the matter at hand. Although you will certainly want to present your company as reliable and capable of upholding the contract, Americans tend to operate more on the foundation of a legal system than one built on personal ties. That is to say, because you are legally bound to comply with the terms of a contract, they do not feel the need to first establish a personal relationship with you.

Once the terms are agreed upon verbally, a legal contract will be drawn up. People generally do not appreciate it if you ask for last-minute concessions. The contract is the final step and is, of course, legally binding. The terms of your agreement will be outlined in great detail and you will be expected to adhere to them.

Making Your Case

Americans pride themselves on being practical. The best way to convince them is to focus on the practicality of your idea or suggestion. You should be able to provide facts that support your argument and a plan for implementation. For example, if you are selling your product to an American company, you will not only need to provide them with information on cost, quality, and technical specifications but also let them know how the product fits into their business and how they can put it to use. However, avoid getting bogged down in details. Remember that Americans are bottom-line oriented and generally prefer outlined points rather than a lengthy lecture on what they consider to be peripheral information; this can be added if, and when, it is necessary.

SPEECHES AND PRESENTATIONS

Whether you are making a speech to a large audience or an informal presentation to a few coworkers, brevity is a virtue. In fact, there is an acronym that is commonly used in courses that teach effective presenting techniques: KISS, which stands for Keep It Short and Simple.

A typical speech or presentation starts out with the speaker or presenter thanking everyone for attending (this often includes a nod to the fact that people have taken time out of their busy schedules to attend) and generally begins on a lighthearted note. For example, the presenter might tell a brief anecdote about an encounter he or she had on the plane trip or say something about a current event, such as "Hey, how 'bout them Cubs?", if the local sports team had an important win last night.

Both speeches and presentations use the following general guideline: tell them what you are going to tell them, tell them, then tell them what you told them. In other words, start with a brief summary of your topic. ("We're introducing a new laundry soap that will bring in $12 million in revenue, and I'm going to tell you how we're going to meet our sales goals.") Follow this with a brief description or explanation. ("This is our three-step plan to launch and market the product.") Then end with another brief summary, this time outlining the major points you made in the body of the presentation. ("Pre-launch advertising, launch in major markets in two months, brand name recognition.")

Making a Presentation

You will notice that there is not a lot of detail in an American presentation. In fact, Americans love bullets! By using bullets, the presenter gives the audience the salient points and avoids overwhelming them with detail. In general, presentations give an overview of the topic, since Americans tend to focus more on the practical implementation of an idea than on the process that led to the idea. Presenters who include too much background information will find their audience fidgeting and checking their watches.

Most presentations are accompanied by overhead projections or computer-generated slideshows; often a copy of these materials is provided to the audience, either before the presentation (so they can follow along and take notes on the handouts) or afterward. Having concise, professional-looking supporting material makes a good impression.

Be sure to leave time at the end of your presentation for questions. Your audience will probably feel quite comfortable asking you questions and even challenging your ideas. It's a good practice to take some time before your presentation to try to think of the questions you might be asked and how you will answer them. Of course, you should be well prepared for your presentation, but there are two skills that every presenter needs: the ability to field questions when you don't know the answer ("I don't have that information in front of me right now, but I will be happy to follow up with you on that.") and the ability to recognize a non-productive question and redirect it appropriately ("That is a valid point, but I think it would be more constructive if we discuss it after this meeting.").

DECISION MAKING

Routine decisions are made at low levels of the organization. Some decisions, such as the goals and direction of the company, are made at the top levels of the organization, but most deals and operations decisions are made by mid-level managers. In addition, most people are given the leeway to make decisions about the routine aspects of their jobs. For example, a customer service representative at the credit card company can usually authorize or deny an increase in your credit line based on your history with the company without consulting a supervisor.

Decisions are often made by individuals or, in cases where other people have to be consulted, by a majority vote; a consensus is not necessary. In other words, you may meet with colleagues to decide on a particular policy or goal and, even though you disagree with the idea in question, if the majority of the team is in favor of it, the decision has been made. You are then expected to comply with the decision, even if you voiced negative input.

The combination of broad decision-making power and the

individualistic or majority-rules approach to decision making means that decisions can be made very quickly. However, the disadvantage is that once the decision has been made, the implementation can be somewhat slow because now other people have to be informed—and often convinced—for the follow through. The flip side of this coin, consensus decision making, encounters initial delays, since many people must not only be consulted but also wooed into agreeing. Still, it has a speedy follow through because everyone is already informed and in agreement.

OFFICE RELATIONSHIPS

The casual atmosphere that exists in most workplaces reflects the relationships that people have with their coworkers. Almost all Americans blend their personal and professional lives to some extent. This may range from discussing their personal lives with colleagues to spending their days off together. At work on Monday, your colleagues may talk about what they did over the weekend. You will hear people

discussing the accomplishments of their children, their social activities, and other aspects of their lives. It's common for coworkers to go out for drinks after work, and younger people often include some of the people they work with in their social circles. Some people even establish friendships with their supervisors and/or subordinates.

The friendly atmosphere in the office can be a bit deceiving, however, since it is expected that you do not let your personal relationship with someone influence your work. If you are a supervisor, for example, and you frequently go out for drinks with one of your subordinates, you still have to be able to reprimand that person when he or she makes a bad blunder.

Romance in the Workplace

When so many hours are spent in the workplace, it is inevitable that occasionally two people who work together also develop a romantic interest in each other. While most organizations would certainly prefer that their employees not mix business and pleasure, most do not have a policy that forbids coworkers from dating. Many, however, do have a policy that discourages romantic relationships between people who are closely linked in the chain of command. In other words, you may not date someone who reports to you or someone to whom you report.

MANAGING

The preferred management style in the United States is more egalitarian than patriarchal in nature. That is, most employees appreciate a manager who acts as a mentor, not one who acts as the head of the family. Employees generally expect to be allowed the independence and latitude to make decisions about their own jobs. The role of the manager, then, is to help the employee set goals and to be available when guidance is necessary. The manager is supposed to help his or her employees realize their potential and continue moving forward as well as keep the whole team working together toward the company's goals.

A manager who is used to a more authoritarian method of management is likely to find that his or her employees resent the interference. An American manager is expected to delegate authority; in fact, most employees relish the challenge of making their own decisions and dislike having to ask permission for every thing that they do.

The egalitarian nature of the management structure means that most managers get their own coffee, read their own e-mail, and type up their own reports. Of course, the higher up in the organization a person is, the more likely he or she is to have an assistant or a secretary to see to these mundane matters. Middle managers, however, must be quite self-sufficient.

As a result of this egalitarian nature, in a few brief moments with a team it may not be obvious who the leader is. There are few clues to go by—everyone is addressed as an equal, there is no formal protocol for introductions, and the seating arrangements are arbitrary. Leaders let their employees speak for themselves, present their own ideas, and so on. Indeed, on the surface, many manager–subordinate relationships seem to be almost friendships. Managers and subordinates are usually on a first-name basis and they may even socialize together. Of course, this level of familiarity can lead to problems if an employee must be disciplined or if there is a perception of favoritism.

EVALUATIONS, FEEDBACK, AND ADVANCEMENT

Most companies have an employee review policy that includes at minimum an annual review; many have three- or six-month reviews as well. An employee will meet with his or her manager to discuss the employee's goals for the review period; when review time rolls around, the employee's accomplishments are measured against the goals.

While employees expect to receive an annual raise, the amount of that raise is often dependent on the accomplishment of goals and job performance, not just putting in time. In general, a 4% cost-of-living raise is the norm; additional percentages are given if the employee has met all of his or her goals or has performed exceptionally.

Evaluations address measurable goals, such as a specified number of sales or cases handled, as well as intangibles, such as the ability to communicate, initiative, and leadership qualities. Employees are generally evaluated by both their managers and their peers. For example, three of your coworkers with whom you work closely may be asked to fill out an evaluation. These, along with your manager's evaluation, are combined for an overall evaluation. Peer reviews are often done anonymously; however, you may be asked which of your coworkers you want to evaluate you.

Feedback, both on formal evaluations and in other areas, is given frankly. Employees are expected to welcome constructive criticism, which will help them improve their job performance. Of course, criticism of any type, constructive or otherwise, is hard to swallow, but Americans are expected to separate professional criticism from personal criticism.

For people from a culture that has a more direct communication style, such as Germany, the American style of giving feedback seems to be too ambiguous. That is, criticism is sandwiched between compliments. For example, a manager might say, "Your technical skills have improved considerably, and your resolution rate is good. However, you need to work on your customer service skills, and you have to start following through better." Even in a less structured environment, you will hear Americans padding the blow with a positive statement before the inevitable "but": "That's not a bad idea, Joe, but . . . ."

For people from cultures that have more indirect communication styles, the American willingness to candidly address problems and shortcomings can seem unduly harsh. However, most Americans would be oblivious to a more subtle approach and, more importantly, would feel that it is a waste of time to "beat around the bush." The compromise, therefore, is to mention the positive as well as the negative to bolster the recipient's confidence while still discussing the problem openly.

Competition for jobs and for advancement in the United States can be fierce. When it's time to decide who gets the promotion, the individual's achievements speak louder than their tenure with the company. It is common for young people to be promoted over their seniors if they have performed better. As in the evaluation of an employee, a person's leadership skills often count for more than his or her technical skills when it comes time to pick someone for promotion. In fact, most company leaders in the United States come up through the ranks of management, marketing, finance, or other "soft skills" departments rather than from the engineering or other technical departments. It stands to reason, therefore, that the only way to get promoted is to make sure that others recognize your contributions. That recognition is usually accomplished by self-advertisement, not by having others tout your accomplishments.

HIRING AND FIRING

If you are going to be in a position to hire and fire employees, it is vital that you familiarize yourself with the legal aspects of this task. For example, federal equal opportunity laws prohibit employers from asking questions that may result in discrimination on the basis of gender, age, physical disability, religion, or sexual orientation. This section is designed to provide general information only; your company's human resources department can give you more information on both your company's policies and applicable laws.

Interviews tend to focus more on accomplishments than on certifications. The interviewee is asked about his or her accomplishments and how he or she can contribute to the company. Hiring is competitive, and potential employees know that in order to make themselves stand out, they must "toot their own horns," so they generally come prepared to impress you with their accomplishments. If you are used to a more subtle, humble approach, applicants may seem boastful, but that is the norm in the United States.

Unless the job is wholly technical, most American companies look for more intangible qualities in their employees, such as leadership ability, strong interpersonal communication skills, and the ability to work in a team. Of course, the person has to be technically able to do their jobs—a computer network specialist has to know about computers, and so on. However, the strongest candidates have more than technical expertise on their side.

In the United States, hiring a family member or friend is frowned upon. The basis of American business is competition and achievement, an environment that leaves little room for nepotism.

Firing someone for cause—because they have done something wrong or if they have not done their job properly—is not particularly difficult. However, if the employee feels he or she has been unjustly fired or if there has been inappropriate behavior on the part of the company, such as sexual harassment, he or she can file a lawsuit against the company.

Layoffs, unfortunately, are not an uncommon occurrence. A company does not need to have federal approval for mass layoffs, and their only obstacle may be union contracts. Generally, companies do give employees a package, usually consisting of some portion of their annual salary and continued benefits.

EIGHT

LAST NOTES

Hopefully this book has given you some insight into the United States and has prepared you for a successful, rewarding relationship with America and Americans. The practical tips contained in this book should help you feel more comfortable as your journey begins, and the information on the American culture will help you navigate as your journey continues.

In addition to the specific information covered in these seven chapters, don't forget these important guidelines for cross-cultural interaction anywhere around the globe:

- Learn about the culture you are visiting. The better you understand the culture, the more prepared you will be to match your skills to their expectations.

- Keep your sense of humor. Things are guaranteed to go wrong now and again, and you will make mistakes. Your best defense is your ability to find humor in the situation.
- And finally, respect other cultures. Just because it's not the way you do things doesn't mean it's wrong.

Good luck in the exciting new environment that awaits you in the United States!

LANGUAGE

It's likely that you already have a strong grasp of the English language if you've already read this book. In order to supplement the English you already know, the "Language" section of this book contains the types of business vocabulary and expressions you will run into everyday when conducting business with Americans. Listen to the words and phrases on the CD and repeat in the pauses provided.

BUSINESS VOCABULARY

accept (to)	boss
account(s)	buy (to)
agenda(s)	capital
asset(s)	close a deal (to)
benefit(s)	cold call(s)
black market	colleague(s)

contract(s)
copyright (©)
deal(s)
economy
embargo(es)
employee(s)
employer(s)
global village
gross domestic
    product (GDP)
gross national
    product (GNP)
guarantee(s)
human resources
    (HR)
income
information
    technology (IT)
interview
issue(s)
item(s)
job(s)
junior executive
labor (labor force)
liquidate (to)

meeting(s)
negotiate (to)
offer(s)
option(s)
presentation(s)
price(s)
product(s)
profit(s)
propose (to)
quality
quantity
reject (to)
résumé
sell (to)
seminar(s)
senior executive
service(s)
specification(s)
stock(s)
supervisor(s)
trademark (™)
training session(s)
union(s)
yield

BUSINESS IDIOMATIC EXPRESSIONS

While working in the United States you may hear some phrases that are unfamiliar to you. The following phrases appear in many every-day business conversations, and so you may want to familiarize yourself with them.

Let's get the ball rolling.	*Let's get started.*
We're making a lot of headway.	*We're making a lot of progress.*
Think outside the box.	*Be more creative. (Think outside the limits.)*
Run it up the flagpole.	*Let everyone know about it.*
I'm between a rock and a hard place.	*I'm in a bad situation with no foreseeable good ending.*
Don't put all your eggs in one basket.	*Don't put all of your resources in the same place.*
I'd like everyone to get on board.	*I'd like everyone to participate and pledge his or her support to the situation.*
I'm playing devil's advocate.	*I'm presenting the opposing argument to the situation.*
Keep me in the loop.	*Keep me informed about the situation.*
They're dragging their heels on this one.	*They're being reluctant and slow to act.*
We'll touch base.	*We'll keep in touch regarding the situation.*
He's given me the green light.	*He's told me it's okay to start work on that.*
I need these reports yesterday.	*I need these reports immediately.*
He's just a flash in the pan.	*He's a person with short-lived accomplishments.*
Put your nose to the grindstone.	*Get to work.*
Get your foot in the door.	*Get a first appointment./Get inside the company.*
It's a catch-22.	*It's a situation where you can't win.*
The company has gone belly up.	*The company has gone bankrupt.*
Just bite the bullet.	*Just accept the unpleasant situation.*
The company is cleaning house.	*The company is laying off a lot of employees.*

We need to put our heads together.	*We need to think together.*
He's got a lot of clout.	*He has a lot of significant influence.*
Is the glass half full or half empty?	*Do you have a positive or negative perception of the situation?*
That's a kick in the pants.	*That's discouraging.*
There's a light at the end of the tunnel.	*There's still hope.*
It's a dog-eat-dog world.	*It's a competitive world.*
We're making inroads.	*We're making progress.*
The project is dead in the water.	*The project is not going anywhere.*
Let's go back to the drawing board.	*Let's start over.*
Let's lay our cards on the table.	*Let's show our plans openly.*
Don't burn your bridges.	*Don't create a situation where you can't go back and change things.*
Keep on your toes.	*Be ready.*
Let's not reinvent the wheel.	*Let's not start from scratch for something for which the work has already been done.*
She's sitting on the fence.	*She's refusing to make a decision.*
When push comes to shove . . .	*When you're forced to make a decision . . .*
She's got plenty on her plate.	*She has a lot of work to do.*
I can't make heads or tails of this.	*I can't understand what this means.*
It's Greek to me.	*I don't understand a bit of it./I'm completely unfamiliar with it.*
That's just a ball-park figure.	*That's just an approximate number.*
We need to strike while the iron is hot.	*We need to act while there is opportunity.*

COMMONLY USED ABBREVIATIONS

ASAP   *as soon as possible*
BTW*   *by the way*
FYI   *for your information*
IMHO* *in my humble opinion*
PC   *politically correct*
RE   *regarding*
TGIF   *thank goodness it's Friday*

*not commonly said aloud as abbreviations

COMPUTER TERMINOLOGY

Computers are a part of business all over the United States, and every day, more companies and individuals come to rely on the computer. As the technology grows, the terminology broadens with it to include a multitude of phrases. Following are several terms that are used frequently when dealing with computers in the workplace.

access privileges—*permission to copy or read information from a network or site*
   You don't have access privileges to that folder. You need a password.
application—*also known as application program; a computer program used for a specific task, such as word processing*
   You will need a spreadsheet application in order to look at the data we sent you.
attachment—*a document added to an e-mail*
   I can't open the attachment you sent because I don't have the right application.
browser—*a computer program such as Explorer or Netscape, used to search the Internet*
   Open the browser and type in the URL of the Web site.
cc—*to send someone a copy of an e-mail or memo (indicated by cc:); comes from "carbon copy," an outdated means of making copies of documents*
   Make sure you cc me on that memo.
crash—*to shut down unexpectedly*
   The computer crashed when I tried to print the document.

cyberspace—*a term coined by science fiction author William Gibson to describe a common area shared by a network of computers; the Internet*

There are many other companies out there in cyberspace with products like ours.

database—*data or information organized into an accessible, searchable collection*

The database contains all the information you need on the client.

dot-com—*a company doing business partially or exclusively on the Internet; the name is taken from the pronunciation of the commercial Internet URL suffix ".com"*

He left our finance company to design Web pages for a **dot-com**.

double-click—*using the mouse to click twice quickly in succession; often used to open a document or folder*

Double-click on the icon to open your word processing application.

download—*to receive data or programs electronically onto your computer's hard drive from another computer or server*

You need to download the file from the server before you can open it.

file—*a collection of electronic data*

The report is in the "Current" file on my hard drive.

hard copy—*copy of a memo or letter on paper, as opposed to the computer-saved data*

I'll need a hard copy of the report as well as a disk.

hard drive—*main storage unit built in to the computer*

There's not enough room on your hard drive; you'll have to save the document to disk.

hardware—*refers to the computer and any external drives*

There is something wrong with the hardware; the computer won't turn on.

HTML (Hypertext Mark-up Language)—*the computer language used to design Web pages*

You have to learn HTML to become a Web designer.

ISP (Internet Service Provider)—*a company that provides access to the World Wide Web and e-mail*

You need to sign up with an ISP before you can use the Internet from home.

laptop—*a portable personal computer*

I'm taking my laptop on the plane to get some work done.

log on—*to gain access to a system or online service*

Can I log on and check my e-mail?

log off—*to terminate a session on a computer server or online service*

Log off when you're finished checking your e-mail.

Mac or Macintosh—*user-friendly computers introduced by Apple Computers in 1984.*

Everyone in our design department works on a Mac.

mailing list—*a service on the Internet one can subscribe to in order to obtain frequent e-mails on a specific topic; can be contributed to by subscribers*

I'm on a mailing list for information on new technologies in the medical sector.

mainframe—*a large, powerful computer that is capable of storing and manipulating much of a corporation's data*

The mainframe is down; we'll have to wait before we can access any of our archived files.

modem—*a piece of equipment that uses the telephone line to transmit data by changing it into signals*

You need a modem in order to get on the Internet.

multimedia—*a program combining text, graphics, audio, and video*

His multimedia presentation really impressed the buyers.

network—*a group of computers hooked up together*

The network serves the entire marketing department.

online—*to be connected to the Internet through a modem*

Go online and look up their Web site.

password—*a word or numbers used to access information not available to the public*

Please enter your password.

PC (personal computer)—*the name given by IBM to their line of microcomputers; this is now used to define all IBM-type computers that are not Macs (see Mac or Macintosh).*

My PC won't run this file; it's a Mac application.

reboot—*to start a computer again*

My computer crashed, so the IT team told me to reboot it.

scroll—*moving a page on the screen up or down using either the scroll bar and arrows or the wheel on the mouse*

Scroll down to the bottom of the page for the copyright information.

search engine—*software used in locating information on the Internet*

Our company's Web page has a search engine so customers can find information on specific products.

server—*main control computer running a set of individual desktop computers*

The server is down, so I can't access my printer.

software—*application programs that run the computer or run using a computer*

You need to buy the software for the spreadsheet program and install it onto your hard drive.

surf the Internet—*to browse through sites on the World Wide Web*

I had some free time, so I decided to surf the Internet for a while.

technical support—*a service provided by software and hardware computer companies to customers; it offers help and instruction on using their products*

I had to call technical support *when I couldn't access any of my files.*

URL (Uniform Resource Locator)—*an address system used by the Internet*

The URL *for the Terra Cognita Web site is www.terracognita.com.*

user-friendly—*describes a system or program that is easy to use, even for a beginner*

Most word-processing programs are user-friendly, *so you shouldn't have many problems.*

Web site—*a group of pages on the World Wide Web used by one person or company*

Check out our Web site *for more information on our product.*

BEFORE YOU GO

Passports. Be sure that each member of your family has one and that each is valid for the length of your assignment. Children should have separate passports; otherwise they will not be allowed to travel alone or with an adult other than their parents, even in an emergency.

Visas. Check with the embassy of any countries you will be in for necessary visas. Requirements vary by country, especially for international relocation. As you travel, don't overlook the fact that some countries require a transit visa for people passing through the country, even if you don't get off your plane or train.

Vaccinations/Inoculations. Check for recommended vaccinations or inoculations for the country you will be living in as well as for any countries you intend to visit. (This is listed on the U.S. Department of State Consular Information Sheet; see "Copies of important documents" below.) The Department of Health and Human Services Office of Public Health Services is able to issue an International Certificate of Vaccination (ICV) containing your personal history of vaccinations. The ICV is approved by the World Health Organization.

Insurance. Make sure that your insurance will cover you while you are abroad. Check now, before you need it. If it won't, do some research to find out how to supplement or change your insurance so that you are adequately covered.

International driver's permits. Although you can use a U.S. or Canadian driver's license in some countries, it is generally advisable to obtain an international driver's permit. This is available from AAA (Automobile Association of America) for a small fee and does not require taking a test. International driver's permits are valid for one year; after that time, you may have to get a local driver's license. Be sure that you get a permit that is valid for the country/countries in which you will be driving.

Pets. Check with the consulate of your host country to find out about restrictions and requirements for bringing pets into the country. Most countries require a health and immunization certificate from a veterinarian; some have quarantine periods upon arrival.

Medical records. Obtain complete medical records for each member of your family. Have one copy on hand for the trip in case of an emergency.

Prescriptions and medications. If you or anyone in your family takes prescription medication, especially those containing narcotics, have your doctor give you a letter stating what the drug is and why it is necessary. Be sure you get a list of the Latin names of all prescription drugs from your doctor, since brand names vary from country to country. Take a six-month supply of any prescription medication, if possible. All medication, prescription or over-the-counter, should be in its original bottle and clearly labeled. Drug and narcotics laws are very strict in many countries, and you do not want to run afoul of them. Ask your dentist if it is advisable to have fluoride treatments, especially for children; most countries do not add fluoride to the water.

School records. If you have chosen a school for your child, you will probably have already made arrangements to forward your child's records. If not, be sure to request a complete set of records to take with you for each child. Don't forget school records, including diplomas and certificates, for yourself or your partner if either one of you might continue your education while you're abroad.

Wills and guardianships. Your personal affairs should be in order before you leave. Your lawyer or a family member should have access to these documents in case of an emergency.

Power of attorney. Assign power of attorney to act in your interest at home, if necessary. (Power of attorney is not permanent and can be nullified when you return, if desired.)

Paying bills. If you have payments that must be made while you're abroad, decide how to handle them before you go. There are several options, including maintaining a checking account at home and paying bills yourself, arranging for your bank to pay them (not all banks offer this service), or having your lawyer, accountant, or a family member pay them.

Copies of important documents. Make two copies of important documents; take one with you and leave one with your lawyer or a family member. Important documents include

- Passport (the pages that contains your passport number and other information)
- Visas, transit visas, and tourist cards
- Driver's license and/or international driving permit
- Insurance card and other information
- International Certificate of Vaccination and medical records

Special needs. If you or anyone in your family has any special needs, check that appropriate facilities and services are available from hotels and airlines. Not all are equipped to deal with infants, persons with physical disabilities, and other concerns such as medication that requires special handling or refrigeration.

Change of address. Be sure to inform all of the necessary people and companies of your change of address. Some companies will assess a service fee for mailing bills and statements internationally. Write to each company, and keep a copy of the notice in case a problem develops and to remind you what bills and statements you should be receiving. Don't forget the following:

- Banks where you are keeping local accounts or have loans
- Credit cards, including department store and gasoline cards
- Stockbroker or stock transfer agent, retirement account agents
- Lawyer
- Accountant
- Insurance company, including homeowners, personal, medical, and life
- Tax offices in any city or state where you have property tax liabilities
- Voter registration office
- Magazines and periodicals
- Alumni associations and professional memberships

Bank letter of reference. It is often difficult to establish banking services in a country where you have no credit history. It will help to have your current bank or credit card write you a letter of good credit. A letter from your local office in your new country that states your salary is also helpful. Some banks now have branches in many countries; you may be able to open an expatriate account at home before you leave that will allow access to bank services worldwide.

Close unnecessary accounts. However, you should leave open one or two key accounts that will provide you with a credit history when you return. Also, make arrangements to terminate telephone service, utility service, garbage collection, newspaper delivery, and other services as necessary.

Inventory. An inventory of all of your belongings is helpful for shipping and insurance purposes. Enlist the help of an appraiser as necessary for items of value.

Packing. Put a card with your name and address inside each piece of luggage and each box being shipped. Don't put your passport in the boxes to be shipped!

CONTACTS & RESOURCES

U.S. Chamber of Commerce

www.uschamber.org
The U.S. Chamber of Commerce is an umbrella organization for the many local chambers of commerce. To find a chamber of commerce in your city, you can check your local yellow pages or visit this Web site, which lists local chambers.

American Chambers of Commerce Abroad (AmCham)

www.uschamber.org/International/default.htm
The U.S. Chamber of Commerce has partnered with business organizations in many countries to create mutually beneficial business relationships. Visit this Web page to learn more about the U.S. Chamber of Commerce's relationship with your country.

World Trade Centers Association

iserve.wtca.org
The World Trade Centers Association is an organization of nearly 300 world trade centers in almost 100 countries, connected to expand global business. Visit their Web site to find a World Trade Center near you.

EMBASSIES AND CONSULATES

The American embassy and consulates in your country, as well as your country's embassy and consulates in the United States, can be invaluable sources of information and business networking.

Embassies and Consulates Worldwide

www.us-immigration.org/consular.htm
This Web site provides a full list of contact information for United States embassies and consulates in countries around the world.

INFORMATION ON THE UNITED STATES

Info USA

usinfo.state.gov/usa/infousa/
Provided by the U.S. Department of State, this authoritative resource is for foreign audiences seeking information about American society, political processes, official U.S. policies and culture.

State Home Pages

www.state.[state abbreviation].us
State home pages provide valuable information on living, working, and staying in each of the 50 states. The home pages of each

U.S. state can be found by using the formula above (the 50 state abbreviations are listed in the "Background" chapter at the beginning of this book).

Immigration and Naturalization Services

www.ins.usdoj.gov

The INS is the main government organ for immigration services in the United States. Their Web site provides information on procedures for applying for visas to enter the United States along with information on immigration services and benefits.

RESOURCES FOR MOVING ABROAD

Video Overseas, Inc.

246 8th Avenue, 2nd floor
New York, NY 10011
Tel: (212) 645-0797
Fax: (212) 242-8144
www.videooverseas.com

Household appliances and electronics that are adapted or manufactured for international use.

Air Animal, Inc. (U.S. and Canada)

4120 West Cypress Street
Tampa, FL 33607-2358
Tel: (800) 635-3448
www.airanimal.com

Information and assistance on moving your pet abroad.

DRIVING AND AUTOMOBILES

U.S. Department of Transportation

400 7th Street, S.W.
Washington, DC 20590
Tel: (202) 366-4000
www.dot.gov
The Department of Transportation Web site contains links to each state's department of motor vehicles.

American Automobile Association (AAA)

www.aaa.com
For information on driving while abroad and international driving permits.

HELPFUL WEB SITES FOR EXPATRIATES

Escape Artist

www.escapeartist.com

Expat Exchange

www.expatexchange.com

CROSS-CULTURAL RESOURCES

Terra Cognita

www.terracognita.com
Videos, books, and audio, as well as Internet training and re-sources for living and working around the world.

METRIC CONVERSIONS

Although a sizing conversion chart can be a step in the right direction, an accurate fit is found only by trying the item on, just as you would at home.

WOMEN'S DRESSES AND SKIRTS

U.S.	4	6	8	10	12	14	16	18
Metric	34	36	38	40	42	44	46	48
British	6	8	10	12	14	16	18	20

WOMEN'S BLOUSES AND SWEATERS

U.S.	4	6	8	10	12	14	16	18	20	22	24
Metric	32	34	36	38	40	42	44	46	48	50	52
British	26	28	30	32	34	36	38	40	42	44	46

WOMEN'S SHOES

U.S.	5	6	7	8	9	10
Metric	36	37	38	39	40	41
British	3½	4½	5½	6½	7½	8½

MEN'S SUITS

U.S.	34	36	38	40	42	44	46	48
Metric	44	46	48	50	52	54	56	58
British	34	36	38	40	42	44	46	48

MEN'S SHIRTS

U.S.	14½	15	15½	16	16½	17	17½	18
Metric	37	38	39	41	42	43	44	45
British	14½	15	15½	16	16½	17	17½	18

MEN'S SHOES

U.S.	7	8	9	10	11	12	13
Metric	39½	41	42	43	44½	46	47
British	6	7	8	9	10	11	12

CHILDREN'S CLOTHING

U.S.	3	4	5	6	6x
Metric	98	104	110	116	122
British	18	20	22	24	26

CHILDREN'S SHOES

U.S.	8	9	10	11	12	13	1	2	3
Metric	24	25	27	28	29	30	32	33	34
British	7	8	9	10	11	12	13	1	2

DISTANCE

1 yard (yd.)	0.914 meters
1 foot (ft.)	0.305 meters
1 inch (in.)	2.54 centimeters
1 mile (mi.)	1.609 kilometers

1 meter	1.094 yards
1 meter	3.279 feet
1 centimeter	0.394 inches
1 kilometer	0.622 miles

SPEED

1 mile per hour (mph)	1.609 kilometers per hour (km/h)
30 mph	48 km/h
55 mph	88 km/h
65 mph	105 km/h
80 mph	128 km/h
100 mph	160 km/h
1 km/h	0.622 mph
55 km/h	34 mph
65 km/h	40 mph
80 km/h	50 mph
100 km/h	62 mph
150 km/h	93 mph

DRY MEASURES

1 pint (pt.)	.551 liter
1 quart (qt.)	1.101 liters
1 liter (l.)	0.908 dry quarts

LIQUID MEASURES

1 fluid ounce	29.57 milliliters
1 pint	0.47 liter
1 quart	0.946 liters
1 gallon	3.785 liters
1 liter	1.057 liquid quarts

WEIGHT

1 ounce (oz.)	28.35 grams
1 pound (lb.)	0.45 kilograms
1 gram (g)	0.035 ounce
1 kilogram (kg)	2.20 pounds

TEMPERATURE

To convert Fahrenheit into Celsius, subtract 32, multiply by 5, and divide by 9.

To convert Celsius into Fahrenheit, multiply by 9, divide by 5, and add 32.

FAHRENHEIT	→ CELSIUS	CELSIUS	→ FAHRENHEIT
-20	-28	-50	-58
-15	-26	-45	-49
-10	-23	-40	-40
-5	-20	-35	-31
0	-17	-30	-22
5	-15	-25	-13
10	-12	-20	-4
15	-9	-15	5
20	-6	-10	14
25	-3	-5	23
30	-1	0	32
35	1	5	41
40	4	10	50
45	7	15	59
50	10	20	68
55	12	25	77
60	15	30	86
65	18	35	95
70	21	40	104
75	23	45	113

FAHRENHEIT → CELSIUS		CELSIUS → FAHRENHEIT	
80	26	50	122
85	29	55	131
90	32	60	140
95	35	65	149
100	37	70	158
105	40	75	167
110	43	80	176
115	46	85	185
120	48	90	194
125	51	95	203
150	65	100	212
175	79	105	221
200	93	110	230
225	107	115	239
250	121	120	248
275	135	125	257
300	148	150	302
325	162	175	347
350	176	200	392
375	190	225	437
400	204	250	482
425	218	275	527
450	232	300	572